LEVIATHAN

VOLUME ONE OF THREE

GRAND TYPE
GRANDTYPECLASSICS.COM

Leviathan

Hobbes, Thomas 1588 – 1679

First Published by Andrew Crooke in 1651

Text set in 18 point Helvetica.
Chapter headings set in Helvetica Neue.

ISBN: 978-1-83412-380-6 Volume One
ISBN: 978-1-83412-381-3 Volume Two
ISBN: 978-1-83412-382-0 Volume Three

LEVIATHAN

VOLUME ONE OF THREE

THOMAS HOBBES

LEVIATHAN OR THE MATTER, FORME, & POWER OF A COMMON-WEALTH ECCLESIASTICAL AND CIVILL

GRAND TYPE CLASSICS

CONTENTS

VOLUME ONE

VOLUME THREE

Dedication

To my most honor'd friend Mr. Francis Godolphin of Godolphin

Honor'd sir.

YOUR MOST WORTHY Brother Mr SIDNEY GODOLPHIN, when he lived, was pleas'd to think my studies something, and otherwise to oblige me, as you know, with reall testimonies of his good opinion, great in themselves, and the greater for the worthinesse of his person. For there is not any vertue that disposeth a man, either to the service of God, or to the service of his Country, to Civill Society, or private Friendship, that did not manifestly appear in his conversation, not as acquired by necessity, or affected upon occasion, but inhaerent, and shining in a generous constitution of his nature. Therefore in honour and gratitude to him, and with devotion to your selfe, I humbly Dedicate unto you this my discourse of Commonwealth. I know not how the world will receive it, nor how it may reflect on those that shall seem to favour it. For in a way beset with those that contend on one side for too great Liberty, and on the other side for too much Authority, 'tis hard to passe between the points of both unwounded. But yet, me thinks, the endeavour to advance the Civill Power, should not be by the Civill Power condemned; nor private men, by reprehending it, declare they think that Power too great. Besides, I speak not of the men, but (in the Abstract) of the

Seat of Power, (like to those simple and unpartiall creatures in the Roman Capitol, that with their noyse defended those within it, not because they were they, but there) offending none, I think, but those without, or such within (if there be any such) as favour them. That which perhaps may most offend, are certain Texts of Holy Scripture, alledged by me to other purpose than ordinarily they use to be by others. But I have done it with due submission, and also (in order to my Subject) necessarily; for they are the Outworks of the Enemy, from whence they impugne the Civill Power. If notwithstanding this, you find my labour generally decryed, you may be pleased to excuse your selfe, and say that I am a man that love my own opinions, and think all true I say, that I honoured your Brother, and honour you, and have presum'd on that, to assume the Title (without your knowledge) of being, as I am,

Sir,

Your most humble, and most obedient servant, Thomas Hobbes.

Paris APRILL 15/25 1651.

The Introduction

NATURE (the art whereby God hath made and governes the world) is by the art of man, as in many other things, so in this also imitated, that it can make an Artificial Animal. For seeing life is but a motion of Limbs, the begining whereof is in some principall part within; why may we not say, that all Automata (Engines that move themselves by springs and wheeles as doth a watch) have an artificiall life? For what is the Heart, but a Spring; and the Nerves, but so many Strings; and the Joynts, but so many Wheeles, giving motion to the whole Body, such as was intended by the Artificer? Art goes yet further, imitating that Rationall and most excellent worke of Nature, Man. For by Art is created that great LEVIATHAN called a COMMON-WEALTH, or STATE, (in latine CIVITAS) which is but an Artificiall Man; though of greater stature and strength than the Naturall, for whose protection and defence it was intended; and in which, the Soveraignty is an Artificiall Soul, as giving life and motion to the whole body; The Magistrates, and other Officers of Judicature and Execution, artificiall Joynts; Reward and Punishment (by which fastned to the seat of the Soveraignty, every joynt and member is moved to performe his duty) are the Nerves, that do the same in the Body Naturall; The Wealth and Riches of all the particular members, are the Strength; Salus Populi (the Peoples Safety) its Businesse; Counsellors, by whom all things needfull for it to know, are suggested unto it, are the Memory; Equity and Lawes, an artificiall Reason and Will; Concord, Health; Sedition, Sicknesse; and Civill War, Death. Lastly, the Pacts and Covenants, by which the parts of this Body Politique were at first made, set together, and united, resemble that Fiat, or the Let Us Make Man, pronounced by God in the Creation.

To describe the Nature of this Artificiall man, I will consider

First the Matter thereof, and the Artificer; both which is Man.

Secondly, How, and by what Covenants it is made; what are the Rights and just Power or Authority of a Soveraigne; and what it is that Preserveth and Dissolveth it.

Thirdly, what is a Christian Common-Wealth.

Lastly, what is the Kingdome of Darkness.

Concerning the first, there is a saying much usurped of late, That Wisedome is acquired, not by reading of Books, but of Men. Consequently whereunto, those persons, that for the most part can give no other proof of being wise, take great delight to shew what they think they have read in men, by uncharitable censures of one another behind their backs. But there is another saying not of late understood, by which they might learn truly to read one another, if they would take the pains; and that is, Nosce Teipsum, Read Thy Self: which was not meant, as it is now used, to countenance, either the barbarous state of men in power, towards their inferiors; or to encourage men of low degree, to a sawcie behaviour towards their betters; But to teach us, that for the similitude of the thoughts, and Passions of one man, to the thoughts, and Passions of another, whosoever looketh into himselfe, and considereth what he doth, when he does Think, Opine, Reason, Hope, Feare, &c, and upon what grounds; he shall thereby read and know, what are the thoughts, and Passions of all other men, upon the like occasions. I say the similitude of Passions, which are the same in all men, Desire, Feare, Hope, &c; not the similitude or The Objects of the Passions, which are the things Desired, Feared, Hoped, &c: for these the constitution individuall, and particular education do so vary, and they are so easie to be kept from our knowledge, that the characters of mans heart, blotted and confounded as they are, with dissembling, lying, counterfeiting, and erroneous doctrines, are legible onely to him that searcheth hearts. And though by mens actions wee do discover their designee sometimes; yet to do it without comparing them with our own, and distinguishing all circumstances, by which the case may come to be altered, is to decypher without a key, and be for the most part deceived, by too much trust, or by too much diffidence; as he that reads, is himselfe a good or evill man.

But let one man read another by his actions never so perfectly, it serves him onely with his acquaintance, which are but few. He that is to govern a whole Nation, must read in himselfe, not this, or that particular man; but Man-kind; which though it be hard to do, harder than to learn any Language, or Science; yet, when I shall have set down my own reading orderly, and perspicuously, the pains left another, will be onely to consider, if he also find not the same in himselfe. For this kind of Doctrine, admitteth no other Demonstration.

PART ONE

OF MAN

CHAPTER ONE

Of Sense

CONCERNING THE Thoughts of man, I will consider them first Singly, and afterwards in Trayne, or dependance upon one another. Singly, they are every one a Representation or Apparence, of some quality, or other Accident of a body without us; which is commonly called an Object. Which Object worketh on the Eyes, Eares, and other parts of mans body; and by diversity of working, produceth diversity of Apparences.

The Originall of them all, is that which we call Sense; (For there is no conception in a mans mind, which hath not at first, totally, or by parts, been begotten upon the organs of Sense.) The rest are derived from that originall.

To know the naturall cause of Sense, is not very necessary to the business now in hand; and I have els-where written of the same at large. Nevertheless, to fill each part of my present method, I will briefly deliver the same in this place.

The cause of Sense, is the Externall Body, or Object, which presseth the organ proper to each Sense, either immediatly, as in the Tast and Touch; or mediately, as in Seeing, Hearing, and Smelling: which pressure, by the mediation of Nerves, and other strings, and membranes of the body, continued inwards to the Brain, and Heart, causeth there a resistance, or counter-pressure, or endeavour of the heart, to deliver it self: which endeavour because Outward, seemeth to be some matter without. And this Seeming, or Fancy, is that which men call sense; and consisteth, as to the Eye, in a Light, or Colour Figured; To the Eare, in a Sound; To the Nostrill, in an Odour; To the Tongue and Palat, in a Savour; and to the rest of the body, in Heat, Cold, Hardnesse, Softnesse, and such other qualities, as we discern by Feeling. All which qualities called Sensible, are in the object that causeth them, but so many several motions of the matter, by which it presseth our organs diversly. Neither in us that are pressed, are they anything els, but divers motions; (for motion, produceth nothing but motion.) But their apparence to us is Fancy, the same waking, that dreaming. And as pressing, rubbing, or striking the Eye, makes us fancy a light; and pressing the Eare, produceth a dinne; so do the bodies also we see, or hear, produce the same by their strong, though unobserved action, For if those Colours, and Sounds, were in the Bodies, or Objects that cause them, they could not bee severed from them, as by glasses, and in Ecchoes by reflection, wee see they are; where we know the thing we see, is in one place; the apparence, in another. And though at some certain distance, the reall, and very object seem invested with the fancy it begets in us; Yet still the object is one thing, the image or fancy is another. So that Sense in all cases, is nothing els but originall fancy, caused (as I have said) by the pressure, that is, by the motion, of externall things upon our Eyes, Eares, and other organs thereunto ordained.

But the Philosophy-schooles, through all the Universities of Christendome, grounded upon certain Texts of Aristotle, teach another doctrine; and say, For the cause of Vision, that the thing seen, sendeth forth on every side a Visible Species(in English) a Visible

Shew, Apparition, or Aspect, or a Being Seen; the receiving whereof into the Eye, is Seeing. And for the cause of Hearing, that the thing heard, sendeth forth an Audible Species, that is, an Audible Aspect, or Audible Being Seen; which entring at the Eare, maketh Hearing. Nay for the cause of Understanding also, they say the thing Understood sendeth forth Intelligible Species, that is, an Intelligible Being Seen; which comming into the Understanding, makes us Understand. I say not this, as disapproving the use of Universities: but because I am to speak hereafter of their office in a Common-wealth, I must let you see on all occasions by the way, what things would be amended in them; amongst which the frequency of insignificant Speech is one.

CHAPTER TWO

Of Imagination

THAT WHEN A THING lies still, unlesse somewhat els stirre it, it will lye still for ever, is a truth that no man doubts of. But that when a thing is in motion, it will eternally be in motion, unless somewhat els stay it, though the reason be the same, (namely, that nothing can change it selfe,) is not so easily assented to. For men measure, not onely other men, but all other things, by themselves: and because they find themselves subject after motion to pain, and lassitude, think every thing els growes weary of motion, and seeks repose of its own accord; little considering, whether it be not some other motion, wherein that desire of rest they find in themselves, consisteth. From hence it is, that the Schooles say, Heavy bodies fall downwards, out of an appetite to rest, and to conserve their nature in that place which is most proper for them; ascribing appetite, and Knowledge of what is good for their conservation, (which is more than man has) to things inanimate absurdly.

When a Body is once in motion, it moveth (unless something els hinder it) eternally; and whatsoever hindreth it, cannot in an instant, but in time, and by degrees quite extinguish it: And as wee see in the water, though the wind cease, the waves give not over rowling for a long time after; so also it happeneth in that motion, which is made in the internall parts of a man, then, when he Sees, Dreams, &c. For after the object is removed, or the eye shut, wee still retain an image of the thing seen, though more obscure than when we see it. And this is it, that Latines call Imagination, from the image made in seeing; and apply the same, though improperly, to all the other senses. But the Greeks call it Fancy; which signifies Apparence, and is as proper to one sense, as to another. Imagination therefore is nothing but Decaying Sense; and is found in men, and many other living Creatures, as well sleeping, as waking.

MEMORY

The decay of Sense in men waking, is not the decay of the motion made in sense; but an obscuring of it, in such manner, as the light of the Sun obscureth the light of the Starres; which starrs do no less exercise their vertue by which they are visible, in the day, than in the night. But because amongst many stroaks, which our eyes, eares, and other organs receive from externall bodies, the predominant onely is sensible; therefore the light of the Sun being predominant, we are not affected with the action of the starrs. And any object being removed from our eyes, though the impression it made in us remain; yet other objects more present succeeding, and working on us, the Imagination of the past is obscured, and made weak; as the voyce of a man is in the noyse of the day. From whence it followeth, that the longer the time is, after the sight, or Sense of any object, the weaker is the Imagination. For the continuall change of mans body, destroyes in time the parts which in sense were moved: So that the distance of time, and of place, hath one and the same effect in us. For as at a distance of place, that which wee look at, appears dimme, and without distinction of the smaller parts; and as Voyces grow weak, and inarticulate: so also after great distance of time, our imagination of the Past is weak; and wee lose(for example) of Cities wee have seen, many particular Streets; and of

Actions, many particular Circumstances. This Decaying Sense, when wee would express the thing it self, (I mean Fancy it selfe,) wee call Imagination, as I said before; But when we would express the Decay, and signifie that the Sense is fading, old, and past, it is called Memory. So that Imagination and Memory, are but one thing, which for divers considerations hath divers names.

Much memory, or memory of many things, is called Experience. Againe, Imagination being only of those things which have been formerly perceived by Sense, either all at once, or by parts at severall times; The former, (which is the imagining the whole object, as it was presented to the sense) is Simple Imagination; as when one imagineth a man, or horse, which he hath seen before. The other is Compounded; as when from the sight of a man at one time, and of a horse at another, we conceive in our mind a Centaure. So when a man compoundeth the image of his own person, with the image of the actions of an other man; as when a man imagins himselfe a Hercules, or an Alexander, (which happeneth often to them that are much taken with reading of Romants) it is a compound imagination, and properly but a Fiction of the mind. There be also other Imaginations that rise in men, (though waking) from the great impression made in sense; As from gazing upon the Sun, the impression leaves an image of the Sun before our eyes a long time after; and from being long and vehemently attent upon Geometricall Figures, a man shall in the dark, (though awake) have the Images of Lines, and Angles before his eyes: which kind of Fancy hath no particular name; as being a thing that doth not commonly fall into mens discourse.

DREAMS

The imaginations of them that sleep, are those we call Dreams. And these also (as all other Imaginations) have been before, either totally, or by parcells in the Sense. And because in sense, the Brain, and Nerves, which are the necessary Organs of sense, are so benummed in sleep, as not easily to be moved by the action of Externall Objects, there can happen in sleep, no Imagination; and therefore no Dreame, but what proceeds from the agitation of the inward parts of mans body; which inward parts, for the connexion they have with the Brayn, and other Organs, when they be distempered, do keep the same in motion; whereby the Imaginations there formerly made, appeare as if a man were waking; saving that the Organs of Sense being now benummed, so as there is no new object, which can master and obscure them with a more vigorous impression, a Dreame must needs be more cleare, in this silence of sense, than are our waking thoughts. And hence it cometh to pass, that it is a hard matter, and by many thought impossible to distinguish exactly between Sense and Dreaming. For my part, when I consider, that in Dreames, I do not often, nor constantly think of the same Persons, Places, Objects, and Actions that I do waking; nor remember so long a trayne of coherent thoughts, Dreaming, as at other times; And because waking I often observe the absurdity of Dreames, but never dream of the absurdities of my waking Thoughts; I am well satisfied, that being awake, I know I dreame not; though when I dreame, I think my selfe awake.

And seeing dreames are caused by the distemper of some of the inward parts of the Body; divers distempers must needs cause different Dreams. And hence it is, that lying cold breedeth Dreams of Feare, and raiseth the thought and Image of some fearfull object (the motion from the brain to the inner parts, and from the inner parts to the Brain being reciprocall:) and that as Anger causeth heat in some parts of the Body, when we are awake; so when we sleep, the over heating of the same parts causeth Anger, and raiseth up in the brain the Imagination of an Enemy. In the same manner; as naturall kindness, when we are awake causeth desire; and desire makes heat in certain other parts of the body; so also, too much heat in those parts, while wee sleep, raiseth in the brain an imagination of some kindness shewn. In summe, our Dreams are the reverse of our waking Imaginations; The motion when we are awake, beginning at one end; and when we Dream, at another.

APPARITIONS OR VISIONS

The most difficult discerning of a mans Dream, from his waking thoughts, is then, when by some accident we observe not that we have slept: which is easie to happen to a man full of fearfull thoughts; and whose conscience is much troubled; and that sleepeth, without the circumstances, of going to bed, or putting off his clothes, as one that noddeth in a chayre. For he that taketh pains, and industriously layes himselfe to sleep, in case any uncouth and exorbitant fancy come unto him, cannot easily think it other than a Dream. We read of Marcus Brutes, (one that had his life given him by Julius Caesar, and was also his favorite, and notwithstanding murthered him,) how at Phillipi, the night before he gave battell to Augustus Caesar, he saw a fearfull apparition, which is commonly related by Historians as a Vision: but considering the circumstances, one may easily judge to have been but a short Dream. For sitting in his tent, pensive and troubled with the horrour of his rash act, it was not hard for him, slumbering in the cold, to dream of that which most affrighted him; which feare, as by degrees it made him wake; so also it must needs make the Apparition by degrees to vanish: And having no assurance that he slept, he could have no cause to think it a Dream, or any thing but a Vision. And this is no very rare Accident: for even they that be perfectly awake, if they be timorous, and supperstitious, possessed with fearfull tales, and alone in the dark, are subject to the like fancies, and believe they see spirits and dead mens Ghosts walking in Churchyards; whereas it is either their Fancy onely, or els the knavery of such persons, as make use of such superstitious feare, to pass disguised in the night, to places they would not be known to haunt.

From this ignorance of how to distinguish Dreams, and other strong Fancies, from vision and Sense, did arise the greatest part of the Religion of the Gentiles in time past, that worshipped Satyres, Fawnes, nymphs, and the like; and now adayes the opinion than rude people have of Fayries, Ghosts, and Goblins; and of the power of Witches. For as for Witches, I think not that their witch craft is any reall power; but yet that they are justly punished, for the false beliefe they have, that they can do such mischiefe, joyned with their purpose to do it if they can; their trade being neerer to a new Religion, than to a Craft or Science. And for Fayries, and walking Ghosts, the opinion of them has I think been on purpose, either taught, or not confuted, to keep in credit the use of Exorcisme, of Crosses, of holy Water, and other such inventions of Ghostly men. Neverthelesse, there is no doubt, but God can make unnaturall Apparitions. But that he does it so often, as men need to feare such things, more than they feare the stay, or change, of the course of Nature, which he also can stay, and change, is no point of Christian faith. But evill men under pretext that God can do any thing, are so bold as to say any thing when it serves their turn, though they think it untrue; It is the part of a wise man, to believe them no further, than right reason makes that which they say, appear credible. If this superstitious fear of Spirits were taken away, and with it, Prognostiques from Dreams, false Prophecies, and many other things depending thereon, by which, crafty ambitious persons abuse the simple people, men would be much more fitted than they are for civill Obedience.

And this ought to be the work of the Schooles; but they rather nourish such doctrine. For (not knowing what Imagination, or the Senses are), what they receive, they teach: some saying, that Imaginations rise of themselves, and have no cause: Others that they rise most commonly from the Will; and that Good thoughts are blown (inspired) into a man, by God; and evill thoughts by the Divell: or that Good thoughts are powred (infused) into a man, by God; and evill ones by the Divell. Some say the Senses receive the Species of things, and deliver them to the Common-sense; and the Common Sense delivers them over to the Fancy, and the Fancy to the Memory, and the Memory to the Judgement, like handing of things from one to another, with many words making nothing understood.

UNDERSTANDING

The Imagination that is raysed in man (or any other creature indued with the faculty of imagining) by words, or other voluntary signes, is that we generally call Understanding; and is common to Man and Beast. For a dogge by custome will understand the call, or the rating of his Master; and so will many other Beasts. That Understanding which is peculiar to man, is the Understanding not onely his will; but his conceptions and thoughts, by the sequell and contexture of the names of things into Affirmations, Negations, and other formes of Speech: And of this kinde of Understanding I shall speak hereafter.

CHAPTER THREE

Of the Consequence or Trayne of Imaginations

BY CONSEQUENCE, or Trayne of Thoughts, I understand that succession of one Thought to another, which is called (to distinguish it from Discourse in words) Mentall Discourse.

When a man thinketh on any thing whatsoever, His next Thought after, is not altogether so casuall as it seems to be. Not every Thought to every Thought succeeds indifferently. But as wee have no Imagination, whereof we have not formerly had Sense, in whole, or in parts; so we have no Transition from one Imagination to another, whereof we never had the like before in our Senses. The reason whereof is this. All Fancies are Motions within us, reliques of those made in the Sense: And those motions that immediately succeeded one another in the sense, continue also together after Sense: In so much as the former comming again to take place, and be praedominant, the later followeth, by coherence of the matter moved, is such manner, as water upon a plain Table is drawn which way any one part of it is guided by the finger. But because in sense, to one and the same thing perceived, sometimes one thing, sometimes another succeedeth, it comes to passe in time, that in the Imagining of any thing, there is no certainty what we shall Imagine next; Onely this is certain, it shall be something that succeeded the same before, at one time or another.

TRAYNE OF THOUGHTS UNGUIDED

This Trayne of Thoughts, or Mentall Discourse, is of two sorts. The first is Unguided, Without Designee, and inconstant; Wherein there is no Passionate Thought, to govern and direct those that follow, to it self, as the end and scope of some desire, or other passion: In which case the thoughts are said to wander, and seem impertinent one to another, as in a Dream. Such are Commonly the thoughts of men, that are not onely without company, but also without care of any thing; though even then their Thoughts are as busie as at other times, but without harmony; as the sound which a Lute out of tune would yeeld to any man; or in tune, to one that could not play. And yet in this wild ranging of the mind, a man may oft-times perceive the way of it, and the dependance of one thought upon another. For in a Discourse of our present civill warre, what could seem more impertinent, than to ask (as one did) what was the value of a Roman Penny? Yet the Cohaerence to me was manifest enough. For the Thought of the warre, introduced the Thought of the delivering up the King to his Enemies; The Thought of that, brought in the Thought of the delivering up of Christ; and that again the Thought of the 30 pence, which was the price of that treason: and thence easily followed that malicious question; and all this in a moment of time; for Thought is quick.

TRAYNE OF THOUGHTS REGULATED

The second is more constant; as being Regulated by some desire, and designee. For the impression made by such things as wee desire, or feare, is strong, and permanent, or, (if it cease for a time,) of quick return: so strong it is sometimes, as to hinder and break our sleep. From Desire, ariseth the Thought of some means we have seen produce the like of that which we ayme at; and from the thought of that, the thought of means to that mean; and so continually, till we come to some beginning within our own power. And because the End, by the greatnesse of the impression, comes often to mind, in case our thoughts begin to wander, they are quickly again reduced into the way: which observed by one of the seven wise men, made him give men this praecept, which is now worne out, Respice Finem; that is to say, in all your actions, look often upon what you would have, as the thing that directs all your thoughts in the way to attain it.

REMEMBRANCE

The Trayn of regulated Thoughts is of two

kinds; One, when of an effect imagined, wee seek the causes, or means that produce it: and this is common to Man and Beast. The other is, when imagining any thing whatsoever, wee seek all the possible effects, that can by it be produced; that is to say, we imagine what we can do with it, when wee have it. Of which I have not at any time seen any signe, but in man onely; for this is a curiosity hardly incident to the nature of any living creature that has no other Passion but sensuall, such as are hunger, thirst, lust, and anger. In summe, the Discourse of the Mind, when it is governed by designee, is nothing but Seeking, or the faculty of Invention, which the Latines call Sagacitas, and Solertia; a hunting out of the causes, of some effect, present or past; or of the effects, of some present or past cause, sometimes a man seeks what he hath lost; and from that place, and time, wherein hee misses it, his mind runs back, from place to place, and time to time, to find where, and when he had it; that is to say, to find some certain, and limited time and place, in which to begin a method of seeking. Again, from thence, his thoughts run over the same places and times, to find what action, or other occasion might make him lose it. This we call Remembrance, or Calling to mind: the Latines call it Reminiscentia, as it were a Re-Conning of our former actions.

Sometimes a man knows a place determinate, within the compasse whereof his is to seek; and then his thoughts run over all the parts thereof, in the same manner, as one would sweep a room, to find a jewell; or as a Spaniel ranges the field, till he find a sent; or as a man should run over the alphabet, to start a rime.

PRUDENCE

Sometime a man desires to know the event of an action; and then he thinketh of some like action past, and the events thereof one after another; supposing like events will follow like actions. As he that foresees what wil become of a Criminal, re-cons what he has seen follow on the like Crime before; having this order of thoughts, The Crime, the Officer, the Prison, the Judge, and the Gallowes. Which kind of thoughts, is called Foresight, and Prudence, or Providence; and sometimes Wisdome; though such conjecture, through the difficulty of observing all circumstances, be very fallacious. But this is certain; by how much one man has more experience of things past, than another; by so much also he is more Prudent, and his expectations the seldomer faile him. The Present onely has a being in Nature; things Past have a being in the Memory onely, but things To Come have no being at all; the Future being but a fiction of the mind, applying the sequels of actions Past, to the actions that are Present; which with most certainty is done by him that has most Experience; but not with certainty enough. And though it be called Prudence, when the Event answereth our Expectation; yet in its own nature, it is but Presumption. For the foresight of things to come, which is Providence, belongs onely to him by whose will they are to come. From him onely, and supernaturally, proceeds Prophecy. The best Prophet naturally is the best guesser; and the best guesser, he that is most versed and studied in the matters he guesses at: for he hath most Signes to guesse by.

SIGNES

A Signe, is the Event Antecedent, of the Consequent; and contrarily, the Consequent of the Antecedent, when the like Consequences have been observed, before: And the oftner they have been observed, the lesse uncertain is the Signe. And therefore he that has most experience in any kind of businesse, has most Signes, whereby to guesse at the Future time, and consequently is the most prudent: And so much more prudent than he that is new in that kind of business, as not to be equalled by any advantage of naturall and extemporary wit: though perhaps many young men think the contrary.

Neverthelesse it is not Prudence that distinguisheth man from beast. There be beasts, that at a year old observe more, and pursue that which is for their good, more prudently, than a child can do at ten.

CONJECTURE OF THE TIME PAST

As Prudence is a Praesumtion of the Future, contracted from the Experience of time Past; So there is a Praesumtion of things Past taken from other things (not future but) past also. For he that hath seen by what courses and degrees, a flourishing State hath first come into civill warre, and then to ruine;

upon the sights of the ruines of any other State, will guesse, the like warre, and the like courses have been there also. But his conjecture, has the same incertainty almost with the conjecture of the Future; both being grounded onely upon Experience.

There is no other act of mans mind, that I can remember, naturally planted in him, so, as to need no other thing, to the exercise of it, but to be born a man, and live with the use of his five Senses. Those other Faculties, of which I shall speak by and by, and which seem proper to man onely, are acquired, and encreased by study and industry; and of most men learned by instruction, and discipline; and proceed all from the invention of Words, and Speech. For besides Sense, and Thoughts, and the Trayne of thoughts, the mind of man has no other motion; though by the help of Speech, and Method, the same Facultyes may be improved to such a height, as to distinguish men from all other living

Creatures.

Whatsoever we imagine, is Finite. Therefore there is no Idea, or conception of anything we call Infinite. No man can have in his mind an Image of infinite magnitude; nor conceive the ends, and bounds of the thing named; having no Conception of the thing, but of our own inability. And therefore the Name of GOD is used, not to make us conceive him; (for he is Incomprehensible; and his greatnesse, and power are unconceivable;) but that we may honour him. Also because whatsoever (as I said before,) we conceive, has been perceived first by sense, either all at once, or by parts; a man can have no thought, representing any thing, not subject to sense. No man therefore can conceive any thing, but he must conceive it in some place; and indued with some determinate magnitude; and which may be divided into parts; nor that any thing is all in this place, and all in another place at the same time; nor that two, or more things can be in one, and the same place at once: for none of these things ever have, or can be incident to Sense; but are absurd speeches, taken upon credit (without any signification at all,) from deceived Philosophers, and deceived, or deceiving Schoolemen.

CHAPTER FOUR

Of Speech

ORIGINALL OF SPEECH

THE INVENTION OF PRINTING, though ingenious, compared with the invention of Letters, is no great matter. But who was the first that found the use of Letters, is not known. He that first brought them into Greece, men say was Cadmus, the sonne of Agenor, King of Phaenicia. A profitable Invention for continuing the memory of time past, and the conjunction of mankind, dispersed into so many, and distant regions of the Earth; and with all difficult, as proceeding from a watchfull observation of the divers motions of the Tongue, Palat, Lips, and other organs of Speech; whereby to make as many differences of characters, to remember them. But the most noble and profitable invention of all other, was that of Speech, consisting of Names or Apellations, and their Connexion; whereby men register their Thoughts; recall them when they are past; and also declare them one to another for mutuall utility and conversation; without which, there had been amongst men, neither Common-wealth, nor Society, nor Contract, nor Peace, no more than amongst Lyons, Bears, and Wolves. The first author of Speech was GOD himselfe, that instructed Adam how to name such creatures as he presented to his sight; For the Scripture goeth no further in this matter. But this was sufficient to direct him to adde more names, as the experience and use of the creatures should give him occasion; and to joyn them in such manner by degrees, as to make himselfe understood; and so by succession of time, so much language might be gotten, as he had found use for; though not so copious, as an Orator or Philosopher has need of. For I do not find any thing in the Scripture, out of which, directly or by consequence can be gathered, that Adam was taught the names of all Figures, Numbers, Measures, Colours, Sounds, Fancies, Relations; much less the names of Words and Speech, as Generall, Speciall, Affirmative, Negative, Interrogative, Optative, Infinitive, all which are usefull; and least of all, of Entity, Intentionality, Quiddity, and other significant words of the School.

But all this language gotten, and augmented by Adam and his posterity, was again lost at the tower of Babel, when by the hand of God, every man was stricken for his rebellion, with an oblivion of his former language. And being hereby forced to disperse themselves into severall parts of the world, it must needs be, that the diversity of Tongues that now is, proceeded by degrees from them, in such manner, as need (the mother of all inventions) taught them; and in tract of time grew every where more copious.

THE USE OF SPEECH

The generall use of Speech, is to transferre our Mentall Discourse, into Verbal; or the Trayne of our Thoughts, into a Trayne of Words; and that for two commodities; whereof one is, the Registring of the Consequences of our Thoughts; which being apt to slip out of our memory, and put us to a new labour, may again be recalled, by such words as they were marked by. So that the first use of names, is to serve for Markes, or Notes of remembrance. Another is, when many use the same words, to signifie (by their connexion and order,) one to another, what they conceive, or think of each matter; and also what they desire, feare, or have any other passion for, and for this use they are called Signes. Speciall uses of Speech are these; First, to Register, what by cogitation, wee find to be the cause of any thing, present or past; and what we find things present or past may produce, or effect: which in summe, is acquiring of Arts. Secondly, to shew to others that knowledge which we have attained; which is, to Counsell, and Teach one another. Thirdly, to make known to others our wills, and purposes, that we may have the mutuall help of one another. Fourthly, to please and delight our selves, and others, by playing with our words, for pleasure or ornament, innocently.

ABUSES OF SPEECH

To these Uses, there are also foure

correspondent Abuses. First, when men register their thoughts wrong, by the inconstancy of the signification of their words; by which they register for their conceptions, that which they never conceived; and so deceive themselves. Secondly, when they use words metaphorically; that is, in other sense than that they are ordained for; and thereby deceive others. Thirdly, when by words they declare that to be their will, which is not. Fourthly, when they use them to grieve one another: for seeing nature hath armed living creatures, some with teeth, some with horns, and some with hands, to grieve an enemy, it is but an abuse of Speech, to grieve him with the tongue, unlesse it be one whom wee are obliged to govern; and then it is not to grieve, but to correct and amend.

The manner how Speech serveth to the remembrance of the consequence of causes and effects, consisteth in the imposing of Names, and the Connexion of them.

NAMES PROPER & COMMON UNIVERSALL

Of Names, some are Proper, and singular to one onely thing; as Peter, John, This Man, This Tree: and some are Common to many things; as Man, Horse, Tree; every of which though but one Name, is nevertheless the name of divers particular things; in respect of all which together, it is called an Universall; there being nothing in the world Universall but Names; for the things named, are every one of them Individual and Singular.

One Universall name is imposed on many things, for their similitude in some quality, or other accident: And whereas a Proper Name bringeth to mind one thing onely; Universals recall any one of those many.

And of Names Universall, some are of more, and some of lesse extent; the larger comprehending the lesse large: and some again of equall extent, comprehending each other reciprocally. As for example, the Name Body is of larger signification than the word Man, and conprehendeth it; and the names Man and Rationall, are of equall extent, comprehending mutually one another. But here wee must take notice, that by a Name is not alwayes understood, as in Grammar, one onely word; but sometimes by circumlocution many words together. For all these words, Hee That In His Actions Observeth The Lawes Of His Country, make but one Name, equivalent to this one word, Just.

By this imposition of Names, some of larger, some of stricter signification, we turn the reckoning of the consequences of things imagined in the mind, into a reckoning of the consequences of Appellations. For example, a man that hath no use of Speech at all, (such, as is born and remains perfectly deafe and dumb,) if he set before his eyes a triangle, and by it two right angles, (such as are the corners of a square figure,) he may by meditation compare and find, that the three angles of that triangle, are equall to those two right angles that stand by it. But if another triangle be shewn him different in shape from the former, he cannot know without a new labour, whether the three angles of that also be equall to the same. But he that hath the use of words, when he observes, that such equality was consequent, not to the length of the sides, nor to any other particular thing in his triangle; but onely to this, that the sides were straight, and the angles three; and that that was all, for which he named it a Triangle; will boldly conclude Universally, that such equality of angles is in all triangles whatsoever; and register his invention in these generall termes, Every Triangle Hath Its Three Angles Equall To Two Right Angles. And thus the consequence found in one particular, comes to be registred and remembred, as a Universall rule; and discharges our mentall reckoning, of time and place; and delivers us from all labour of the mind, saving the first; and makes that which was found true Here, and Now, to be true in All Times and Places.

But the use of words in registring our thoughts, is in nothing so evident as in Numbering. A naturall foole that could never learn by heart the order of numerall words, as One, Two, and Three, may observe every stroak of the Clock, and nod to it, or say one, one, one; but can never know what houre it strikes. And it seems, there was a time when those names of number were not in use; and men were fayn to apply their fingers of one or both hands, to those things they desired to keep account of; and that thence it proceeded, that now our numerall words are but ten, in any Nation, and in some but five, and then they begin again. And he that can tell ten, if he recite them out of order, will lose himselfe, and not know when he has done: Much lesse will he be able to add, and substract, and performe all other operations of Arithmetique. So that without words, there is no possibility of reckoning of Numbers; much lesse of Magnitudes, of Swiftnesse, of Force, and other things, the reckonings whereof are necessary to the being, or well-being of man-kind.

When two Names are joyned together into a Consequence, or Affirmation; as thus, A Man Is A Living Creature; or thus, If He Be A Man, He Is A Living Creature, If the later name Living Creature, signifie all that the former name Man signifieth, then the affirmation, or consequence is True; otherwise False. For True and False are attributes of Speech, not of things. And where Speech in not, there is neither Truth nor Falshood. Errour there may be, as when wee expect that which shall not be; or suspect what has not been: but in neither case can a man be charged with Untruth.

Seeing then that Truth consisteth in the right ordering of names in our affirmations, a man that seeketh precise Truth, had need to remember what every name he uses stands for; and to place it accordingly; or els he will find himselfe entangled in words, as a bird in lime-twiggs; the more he struggles, the more belimed. And therefore in Geometry, (which is the onely Science that it hath pleased God hitherto to bestow on mankind,) men begin at settling the significations of their words; which settling of significations, they call Definitions; and place them in the beginning of their reckoning.

By this it appears how necessary it is for any man that aspires to true Knowledge, to examine the Definitions of former Authors; and either to correct them, where they are negligently set down; or to make them himselfe. For the errours of Definitions multiply themselves, according as the reckoning proceeds; and lead men into absurdities, which at last they see, but cannot avoyd, without reckoning anew from the beginning; in which lyes the foundation of their errours. From whence it happens, that they which trust to books, do as they that cast up many little summs into a greater, without considering whether those little summes were rightly cast up or not; and at last finding the errour visible, and not mistrusting their first grounds, know not which way to cleere themselves; but spend time in fluttering over their bookes; as birds that entring by the chimney, and finding themselves inclosed in a chamber, flitter at the false light of a glasse window, for want of wit to consider which way they came in. So that in the right Definition of Names, lyes the first use of Speech; which is the Acquisition of Science: And in wrong, or no Definitions' lyes the first abuse; from which proceed all false and senslesse Tenets; which make those men that take their instruction from the authority of books, and not from their own meditation, to be as much below the condition of ignorant men, as men endued with true Science are above it. For between true Science, and erroneous Doctrines, Ignorance is in the middle. Naturall sense and imagination, are not subject to absurdity. Nature it selfe cannot erre: and as men abound in copiousnesse of language; so they become more wise, or more mad than ordinary. Nor is it possible without Letters for any man to become either excellently wise, or (unless his memory be hurt by disease, or ill constitution of organs) excellently foolish. For words are wise mens counters, they do but reckon by them: but they are the mony of fooles, that value them by the authority of an Aristotle, a Cicero, or a Thomas, or any other Doctor whatsoever, if but a man.

SUBJECT TO NAMES

Subject To Names, is whatsoever can enter into, or be considered in an account; and be added one to another to make a summe; or substracted one from another, and leave a remainder. The Latines called Accounts of mony Rationes, and accounting, Ratiocinatio: and that which we in bills or books of account call Items, they called Nomina; that is, Names: and thence it seems to proceed, that they extended the word Ratio, to the faculty of Reckoning in all other things. The Greeks have but one word Logos, for both Speech and Reason; not that they thought there was no Speech without Reason; but no Reasoning without Speech: And the act of reasoning they called syllogisme; which signifieth summing up of the consequences of one saying to another. And because the same things may enter into account for divers accidents; their names are (to shew that diversity) diversly wrested, and diversified. This diversity of names may be reduced to foure generall heads.

First, a thing may enter into account for Matter, or Body; as Living, Sensible, Rationall, Hot, Cold, Moved, Quiet; with all which names the word Matter, or Body is understood; all such, being names of Matter.

Secondly, it may enter into account, or be

considered, for some accident or quality, which we conceive to be in it; as for Being Moved, for Being So Long, for Being Hot, &c; and then, of the name of the thing it selfe, by a little change or wresting, wee make a name for that accident, which we consider; and for Living put into account Life; for Moved, Motion; for Hot, Heat; for Long, Length, and the like. And all such Names, are the names of the accidents and properties, by which one Matter, and Body is distinguished from another. These are called Names Abstract; Because Severed (not from Matter, but) from the account of Matter.

Thirdly, we bring into account, the Properties of our own bodies, whereby we make such distinction: as when any thing is Seen by us, we reckon not the thing it selfe; but the Sight, the Colour, the Idea of it in the fancy: and when any thing is Heard, wee reckon it not; but the Hearing, or Sound onely, which is our fancy or conception of it by the Eare: and such are names of fancies.

Fourthly, we bring into account, consider, and give names, to Names themselves, and to Speeches: For, Generall, Universall, Speciall, Oequivocall, are names of Names. And Affirmation, Interrogation, Commandement, Narration, Syllogisme, Sermon, Oration, and many other such, are names of Speeches.

USE OF NAMES POSITIVE

And this is all the variety of Names Positive; which are put to mark somewhat which is in Nature, or may be feigned by the mind of man, as Bodies that are, or may be conceived to be; or of bodies, the Properties that are, or may be feigned to be; or Words and Speech.

NEGATIVE NAMES WITH THEIR USES

There be also other Names, called

Negative; which are notes to signifie that a word is not the name of the thing in question; as these words Nothing, No Man, Infinite, Indocible, Three Want Foure, and the like; which are nevertheless of use in reckoning, or in correcting of reckoning; and call to mind our past cogitations, though they be not names of any thing; because they make us refuse to admit of Names not rightly used.

WORDS INSIGNIFICANT

All other names, are but insignificant sounds; and those of two sorts. One, when they are new, and yet their meaning not explained by Definition; whereof there have been aboundance coyned by Schoole-men, and pusled Philosophers.

Another, when men make a name of two Names, whose significations are contradictory and inconsistent; as this name, an Incorporeall Body, or (which is all one) an

Incorporeall Substance, and a great number more. For whensoever any affirmation is false, the two names of which it is composed, put together and made one, signifie nothing at all. For example if it be a false affirmation to say A Quadrangle Is Round, the word Round Quadrangle signifies nothing; but is a meere sound. So likewise if it be false, to say that vertue can be powred, or blown up and down; the words In-powred Vertue, In-blown Vertue, are as absurd and insignificant, as a Round Quadrangle. And therefore you shall hardly meet with a senselesse and insignificant word, that is not made up of some Latin or Greek names. A Frenchman seldome hears our Saviour called by the name of Parole, but by the name of Verbe often; yet Verbe and Parole differ no more, but that one is Latin, the other French.

UNDERSTANDING

When a man upon the hearing of any

Speech, hath those thoughts which the words of that Speech, and their connexion, were ordained and constituted to signifie; Then he is said to understand it; Understanding being nothing els, but conception caused by Speech. And therefore if Speech be peculiar to man (as for ought I know it is,) then is Understanding peculiar to him also. And therefore of absurd and false affirmations, in case they be universall, there can be no Understanding; though many think they understand, then, when they do but repeat the words softly, or con them in their mind.

What kinds of Speeches signifie the Appetites, Aversions, and Passions of mans mind; and of their use and abuse, I shall speak when I have spoken of the Passions.

INCONSTANT NAMES

The names of such things as affect us, that is, which please, and displease us, because all men be not alike affected with the same thing, nor the same man at all times, are in the common discourses of men, of Inconstant signification. For seeing all names are imposed to signifie our conceptions; and all our affections are but conceptions; when we conceive the same things differently, we can hardly avoyd different naming of them. For though the nature of that we conceive, be the same; yet the diversity of our reception of it, in respect of different constitutions of body, and prejudices of opinion, gives everything a tincture of our different passions. And therefore in reasoning, a man bust take heed of words; which besides the signification of what we imagine of their nature, disposition, and interest of the speaker; such as are the names of Vertues, and Vices; For one man calleth Wisdome, what another calleth Feare; and one Cruelty, what another Justice; one Prodigality, what another Magnanimity; one Gravity, what another Stupidity, &c.

And therefore such names can never be true grounds of any ratiocination. No more can Metaphors, and Tropes of speech: but these are less dangerous, because they profess their inconstancy; which the other do not.

CHAPTER FIVE

Of Reason, and Science

REASON WHAT IT IS

WHEN A MAN REASONETH, hee does nothing els but conceive a summe totall, from Addition of parcels; or conceive a Remainder, from Substraction of one summe from another: which (if it be done by Words,) is conceiving of the consequence of the names of all the parts, to the name of the whole; or from the names of the whole and one part, to the name of the other part. And though in some things, (as in numbers,) besides Adding and Substracting, men name other operations, as Multiplying and Dividing; yet they are the same; for Multiplication, is but Addition together of things equall; and Division, but Substracting of one thing, as often as we can. These operations are not incident to Numbers onely, but to all manner of things that can be added together, and taken one out of another. For as Arithmeticians teach to adde and substract in Numbers; so the Geometricians teach the same in Lines, Figures (solid and superficiall,) Angles, Proportions, Times, degrees of Swiftnesse, Force, Power, and the like; The Logicians teach the same in Consequences Of Words; adding together Two Names, to make an Affirmation; and Two Affirmations, to make a syllogisme; and Many syllogismes to make a Demonstration; and from the Summe, or Conclusion of a syllogisme, they substract one Proposition, to finde the other. Writers of Politiques, adde together Pactions, to find mens Duties; and Lawyers, Lawes and Facts, to find what is Right and Wrong in the actions of private men. In summe, in what matter soever there is place for Addition and Substraction, there also is place for Reason; and where these have no place, there Reason has nothing at all to do.

REASON DEFINED

Out of all which we may define, (that is to say determine,) what that is, which is meant by this word Reason, when wee reckon it amongst the Faculties of the mind. For Reason, in this sense, is nothing but Reckoning (that is, Adding and Substracting) of the Consequences of generall names agreed upon, for the Marking and Signifying of our thoughts; I say Marking them, when we reckon by our selves; and Signifying, when we demonstrate, or approve our reckonings to other men.

RIGHT REASON WHERE

And as in Arithmetique, unpractised men must, and Professors themselves may often erre, and cast up false; so also in any other subject of Reasoning, the ablest, most attentive, and most practised men, may deceive themselves, and inferre false Conclusions; Not but that Reason it selfe is always Right Reason, as well as Arithmetique is a certain and infallible art: But no one mans Reason, nor the Reason of any one number of men, makes the certaintie; no more than an account is therefore well cast up, because a great many men have unanimously approved it. And therfore, as when there is a controversy in an account, the parties must by their own accord, set up for right Reason, the Reason of some Arbitrator, or Judge, to whose sentence they will both stand, or their controversie must either come to blowes, or be undecided, for want of a right Reason constituted by Nature; so is it also in all debates of what kind soever: And when men that think themselves wiser than all others, clamor and demand right Reason for judge; yet seek no more, but that things should be determined, by no other mens reason but their own, it is as intolerable in the society of men, as it is in play after trump is turned, to use for trump on every occasion, that suite whereof they have most in their hand. For they do nothing els, that will have every of their passions, as it comes to bear sway in them, to be taken for right Reason, and that in their own controversies: bewraying their want of right Reason, by the claym they lay to it.

THE USE OF REASON

The Use and End of Reason, is not the

finding of the summe, and truth of one, or a few consequences, remote from the first definitions, and settled significations of names; but to begin at these; and proceed from one consequence to another. For there can be no certainty of the last Conclusion, without a certainty of all those Affirmations and Negations, on which it was grounded, and inferred. As when a master of a family, in taking an account, casteth up the summs of all the bills of expence, into one sum; and not regarding how each bill is summed up, by those that give them in account; nor what it is he payes for; he advantages himselfe no more, than if he allowed the account in grosse, trusting to every of the accountants skill and honesty; so also in Reasoning of all other things, he that takes up conclusions on the trust of Authors, and doth not fetch them from the first Items in every Reckoning, (which are the significations of names settled by definitions), loses his labour; and does not know any thing; but onely beleeveth.

OF ERROR AND ABSURDITY

When a man reckons without the use of words, which may be done in particular things, (as when upon the sight of any one thing, wee conjecture what was likely to have preceded, or is likely to follow upon it;) if that which he thought likely to follow, followes not; or that which he thought likely to have preceded it, hath not preceded it, this is called ERROR; to which even the most prudent men are subject. But when we Reason in Words of generall signification, and fall upon a generall inference which is false; though it be commonly called Error, it is indeed an ABSURDITY, or senseless Speech. For Error is but a deception, in presuming that somewhat is past, or to come; of which, though it were not past, or not to come; yet there was no impossibility discoverable. But when we make a generall assertion, unlesse it be a true one, the possibility of it is unconceivable. And words whereby we conceive nothing but the sound, are those we call Absurd, insignificant, and Non-sense. And therefore if a man should talk to me of a Round Quadrangle; or Accidents Of Bread In Cheese; or Immaterial Substances; or of A Free Subject; A Free Will; or any Free, but free from being hindred by opposition, I should not say he were in an Errour; but that his words were without meaning; that is to say, Absurd.

I have said before, (in the second chapter,) that a Man did excell all other Animals in this faculty, that when he conceived any thing whatsoever, he was apt to enquire the consequences of it, and what effects he could do with it. And now I adde this other degree of the same excellence, that he can by words reduce the consequences he findes to generall Rules, called Theoremes, or Aphorismes; that is, he can Reason, or reckon, not onely in number; but in all other things, whereof one may be added unto, or substracted from another.

But this priviledge, is allayed by another; and that is, by the priviledge of Absurdity; to which no living creature is subject, but man onely. And of men, those are of all most subject to it, that professe Philosophy. For it is most true that Cicero sayth of them somewhere; that there can be nothing so absurd, but may be found in the books of Philosophers. And the reason is manifest. For there is not one of them that begins his ratiocination from the Definitions, or Explications of the names they are to use; which is a method that hath been used onely in Geometry; whose Conclusions have thereby been made indisputable.

CAUSES OF ABSURDITIE

The first cause of Absurd conclusions I ascribe to the want of Method; in that they begin not their Ratiocination from Definitions; that is, from settled significations of their words: as if they could cast account, without knowing the value of the numerall words, One, Two, and Three.

And whereas all bodies enter into account upon divers considerations, (which I have mentioned in the precedent chapter;) these considerations being diversly named, divers absurdities proceed from the confusion, and unfit connexion of their names into assertions. And therefore

The second cause of Absurd assertions, I ascribe to the giving of names of Bodies, to Accidents; or of Accidents, to Bodies; As they do, that say, Faith Is Infused, or Inspired; when nothing can be Powred, or Breathed into any thing, but body; and that, Extension is Body; that Phantasmes are Spirits, &c.

The third I ascribe to the giving of the names of the Accidents of Bodies Without Us, to the Accidents of our Own Bodies; as they do that say, the Colour Is In The Body; The Sound Is In The Ayre, &c.

The fourth, to the giving of the names of Bodies, to Names, or Speeches; as they do that say, that There Be Things Universall; that A Living Creature Is Genus, or A Generall Thing, &c.

The fifth, to the giving of the names of Accidents, to Names and Speeches; as they do that say, The Nature Of A Thing Is In Its Definition; A Mans Command Is His Will; and the like.

The sixth, to the use of Metaphors, Tropes, and other Rhetoricall figures, in stead of words proper. For though it be lawfull to say, (for example) in common speech, The Way Goeth, Or Leadeth Hither, Or Thither, The Proverb Sayes This Or That (whereas wayes cannot go, nor Proverbs speak;) yet in reckoning, and seeking of truth, such speeches are not to be admitted.

The seventh, to names that signifie nothing; but are taken up, and learned by rote from the Schooles, as Hypostatical, Transubstantiate, Consubstantiate, Eternal-now, and the like canting of Schoole-men.

To him that can avoyd these things, it is not easie to fall into any absurdity, unlesse it be by the length of an account; wherein he may perhaps forget what went before. For all men by nature reason alike, and well, when they have good principles. For who is so stupid, as both to mistake in Geometry, and also to persist in it, when another detects his error to him?

SCIENCE

By this it appears that Reason is not as Sense, and Memory, borne with us; nor gotten by Experience onely; as Prudence is; but attayned by Industry; first in apt imposing of Names; and secondly by getting a good and orderly Method in proceeding from the Elements, which are Names, to Assertions made by Connexion of one of them to another; and so to syllogismes, which are the Connexions of one Assertion to another, till we come to a knowledge of all the Consequences of names appertaining to the subject in hand; and that is it, men call SCIENCE. And whereas Sense and Memory are but knowledge of Fact, which is a thing past, and irrevocable; Science is the knowledge of Consequences, and dependance of one fact upon another: by which, out of that we can presently do, we know how to do something els when we will, or the like, another time; Because when we see how any thing comes about, upon what causes, and by what manner; when the like causes come into our power, wee see how to make it produce the like effects.

Children therefore are not endued with Reason at all, till they have attained the use of Speech: but are called Reasonable Creatures, for the possibility apparent of having the use of Reason in time to come. And the most part of men, though they have the use of Reasoning a little way, as in numbring to some degree; yet it serves them to little use in common life; in which they govern themselves, some better, some worse, according to their differences of experience, quicknesse of memory, and inclinations to severall ends; but specially according to good or evill fortune, and the errors of one another. For as for Science, or certain rules of their actions, they are so farre from it, that they know not what it is. Geometry they have thought Conjuring: but for other Sciences, they who have not been taught the beginnings, and some progresse in them, that they may see how they be acquired and generated, are in this point like children, that having no thought of generation, are made believe by the women, that their brothers and sisters are not born, but found in the garden.

But yet they that have no Science, are in better, and nobler condition with their naturall Prudence; than men, that by mis-reasoning, or by trusting them that reason wrong, fall upon false and absurd generall rules. For ignorance of causes, and of rules, does not set men so farre out of their way, as relying on false rules, and taking for causes of what they aspire to, those that are not so, but rather causes of the contrary.

To conclude, The Light of humane minds is Perspicuous Words, but by exact definitions first snuffed, and purged from ambiguity; Reason is the Pace; Encrease of Science, the Way; and the Benefit of man-kind, the End. And on the contrary, Metaphors, and senslesse and ambiguous words, are like Ignes Fatui; and reasoning upon them, is wandering amongst innumerable absurdities; and their end, contention, and sedition, or contempt.

PRUDENCE & SAPIENCE, WITH THEIR DIFFERENCE

As, much Experience, is Prudence; so, is much Science, Sapience. For though wee usually have one name of Wisedome for them both; yet the Latines did always distinguish between Prudentia and Sapientia, ascribing the former to Experience, the later to Science. But to make their difference appeare more cleerly, let us suppose one man endued with an excellent naturall use, and dexterity in handling his armes; and another to have added to that dexterity, an acquired Science, of where he can offend, or be offended by his adversarie, in every possible posture, or guard: The ability of the former, would be to the ability of the later, as Prudence to Sapience; both usefull; but the later infallible. But they that trusting onely to the authority of books, follow the blind blindly, are like him that trusting to the false rules of the master of fence, ventures praesumptuously upon an adversary, that either kills, or disgraces him.

SIGNES OF SCIENCE

The signes of Science, are some, certain

and infallible; some, uncertain. Certain, when he that pretendeth the Science of any thing, can teach the same; that is to say, demonstrate the truth thereof perspicuously to another: Uncertain, when onely some particular events answer to his pretence, and upon many occasions prove so as he sayes they must. Signes of prudence are all uncertain; because to observe by experience, and remember all circumstances that may alter the successe, is impossible. But in any businesse, whereof a man has not infallible Science to proceed by; to forsake his own natural judgement, and be guided by generall sentences read in Authors, and subject to many exceptions, is a signe of folly, and generally scorned by the name of Pedantry. And even of those men themselves, that in Councells of the Common-wealth, love to shew their reading of Politiques and History, very few do it in their domestique affaires, where their particular interest is concerned; having Prudence enough for their private affaires: but in publique they study more the reputation of their owne wit, than the successe of anothers businesse.

CHAPTER SIX

Of the Interiour Beginnings of Voluntary Motions Commonly Called the Passions. And the Speeches by which they are Expressed

MOTION VITALL AND ANIMAL

THERE BE IN ANIMALS, two sorts of Motions peculiar to them: One called Vitall; begun in generation, and continued without interruption through their whole life; such as are the Course of the Bloud, the Pulse, the Breathing, the Concoctions, Nutrition, Excretion, &c; to which Motions there needs no help of Imagination: The other in Animal Motion, otherwise called Voluntary Motion; as to Go, to Speak, to Move any of our limbes, in such manner as is first fancied in our minds. That Sense, is Motion in the organs and interiour parts of mans body, caused by the action of the things we See, Heare, &c.; And that Fancy is but the Reliques of the same Motion, remaining after Sense, has been already sayd in the first and second Chapters. And because Going, Speaking, and the like Voluntary motions, depend alwayes upon a precedent thought of Whither, Which Way, and What; it is evident, that the Imagination is the first internall beginning of all Voluntary Motion. And although unstudied men, doe not conceive any motion at all to be there, where the thing moved is invisible; or the space it is moved in, is (for the shortnesse of it) insensible; yet that doth not hinder, but that such Motions are. For let a space be never so little, that which is moved over a greater space, whereof that little one is part, must first be moved over that. These small beginnings of Motion, within the body of Man, before they appear in walking, speaking, striking, and other visible actions, are commonly called ENDEAVOUR.

ENDEAVOUR; APPETITE; DESIRE; HUNGER; THIRST; AVERSION

This Endeavour, when it is toward something which causes it, is called APPETITE, or DESIRE; the later, being the generall name; and the other, oftentimes restrayned to signifie the Desire of Food, namely Hunger and Thirst. And when the Endeavour is fromward something, it is generally called AVERSION. These words Appetite, and Aversion we have from the Latines; and they both of them signifie the motions, one of approaching, the other of retiring. So also do the Greek words for the same, which are orme and aphorme. For nature it selfe does often presse upon men those truths, which afterwards, when they look for somewhat beyond Nature, they stumble at. For the Schooles find in meere Appetite to go, or move, no actuall Motion at all: but because some Motion they must acknowledge, they call it Metaphoricall Motion; which is but an absurd speech; for though Words may be called metaphoricall; Bodies, and Motions cannot.

That which men Desire, they are also sayd to LOVE; and to HATE those things, for which they have Aversion. So that Desire, and Love, are the same thing; save that by Desire, we alwayes signifie the Absence of the object; by Love, most commonly the Presence of the same. So also by Aversion, we signifie the Absence; and by Hate, the Presence of the Object.

Of Appetites, and Aversions, some are born with men; as Appetite of food, Appetite of excretion, and exoneration, (which may also and more properly be called Aversions, from somewhat they feele in their Bodies;) and some other Appetites, not many. The rest, which are Appetites of particular things, proceed from Experience, and triall of their effects upon themselves, or other men. For of things wee know not at all, or believe not to be, we can have no further Desire, than to tast and try. But Aversion wee have for things, not onely which we know have hurt us; but also that we do not know whether they will hurt us, or not.

CONTEMPT

Those things which we neither Desire, nor Hate, we are said to Contemne: CONTEMPT being nothing els but an immobility, or contumacy of the Heart, in resisting the action of certain things; and proceeding from that the Heart is already moved otherwise, by either more potent objects; or from want of experience of them.

And because the constitution of a mans Body, is in continuall mutation; it is impossible that all the same things should alwayes cause in him the same Appetites, and aversions: much lesse can all men consent, in the Desire of almost any one and the same Object.

GOOD EVILL

But whatsoever is the object of any mans Appetite or Desire; that is it, which he for his part calleth Good: And the object of his Hate, and Aversion, evill; And of his contempt, Vile, and Inconsiderable. For these words of Good, evill, and Contemptible, are ever used with relation to the person that useth them: There being nothing simply and absolutely so; nor any common Rule of Good and evill, to be taken from the nature of the objects themselves; but from the Person of the man (where there is no Common-wealth;) or, (in a Common-wealth,) From the Person that representeth it; or from an Arbitrator or Judge, whom men disagreeing shall by consent set up, and make his sentence the Rule thereof.

PULCHRUM TURPE; DELIGHTFULL PROFITABLE; UNPLEASANT UNPROFITABLE

The Latine Tongue has two words, whose significations approach to those of Good and Evill; but are not precisely the same; And those are Pulchrum and Turpe. Whereof the former signifies that, which by some apparent signes promiseth Good; and the later, that, which promiseth evill. But in our Tongue we have not so generall names to expresse them by. But for Pulchrum, we say in some things, Fayre; in other Beautifull, or Handsome, or Gallant, or Honourable, or

Comely, or Amiable; and for Turpe, Foule, Deformed, Ugly, Base, Nauseous, and the like, as the subject shall require; All which words, in their proper places signifie nothing els, but the Mine, or Countenance, that promiseth Good and evill. So that of Good there be three kinds; Good in the Promise, that is Pulchrum; Good in Effect, as the end desired, which is called Jucundum, Delightfull; and Good as the Means, which is called Utile, Profitable; and as many of evill: For evill, in Promise, is that they call Turpe; evill in Effect, and End, is Molestum, Unpleasant, Troublesome; and evill in the Means, Inutile, Unprofitable, Hurtfull.

DELIGHT DISPLEASURE

As, in Sense, that which is really within us, is (As I have sayd before) onely Motion, caused by the action of externall objects, but in apparence; to the Sight, Light and Colour; to the Eare, Sound; to the Nostrill, Odour,

&c: so, when the action of the same object is continued from the Eyes, Eares, and other organs to the Heart; the real effect there is nothing but Motion, or Endeavour; which consisteth in Appetite, or Aversion, to, or from the object moving. But the apparence, or sense of that motion, is that wee either call DELIGHT, or TROUBLE OF MIND.

PLEASURE OFFENCE

This Motion, which is called Appetite, and for the apparence of it Delight, and Pleasure, seemeth to be, a corroboration of Vitall motion, and a help thereunto; and therefore such things as caused Delight, were not improperly called Jucunda, (A Juvando,) from helping or fortifying; and the contrary, Molesta, Offensive, from hindering, and troubling the motion vitall.

Pleasure therefore, (or Delight,) is the apparence, or sense of Good; and Molestation or Displeasure, the apparence, or sense of evill. And consequently all Appetite, Desire, and Love, is accompanied with some Delight more or lesse; and all Hatred, and Aversion, with more or lesse Displeasure and Offence.

PLEASURES OF SENSE; PLEASURES OF THE MIND; JOY PAINE GRIEFE

Of Pleasures, or Delights, some arise from the sense of an object Present; And those may be called Pleasures Of Sense, (The word Sensuall, as it is used by those onely that condemn them, having no place till there be Lawes.) Of this kind are all Onerations and Exonerations of the body; as also all that is pleasant, in the Sight, Hearing, Smell, Tast, Or Touch; Others arise from the Expectation, that proceeds from foresight of the End, or Consequence of things; whether those things in the Sense Please or Displease: And these are Pleasures Of The Mind of him that draweth those consequences; and are generally called JOY. In the like manner, Displeasures, are some in the Sense, and called PAYNE; others, in the Expectation of consequences, and are called GRIEFE.

These simple Passions called Appetite, Desire, Love, Aversion, Hate, Joy, and griefe, have their names for divers considerations diversified. As first, when they one succeed another, they are diversly called from the opinion men have of the likelihood of attaining what they desire. Secondly, from the object loved or hated. Thirdly, from the consideration of many of them together. Fourthly, from the Alteration or succession it selfe.

Hope– For Appetite with an opinion of attaining, is called HOPE.

Despaire–The same, without such opinion, DESPAIRE.

Feare– Aversion, with opinion of Hurt from the object, FEARE.

Courage–The same, with hope of avoyding

that Hurt by resistance, COURAGE.

Anger– Sudden Courage, ANGER.

Confidence– Constant Hope, CONFIDENCE of our selves.

Diffidence– Constant Despayre, DIFFIDENCE of our selves.

Indignation– Anger for great hurt done to another, when we conceive the same to be done by Injury, INDIGNATION.

Benevolence– Desire of good to another, BENEVOLENCE, GOOD WILL, CHARITY. If to man generally, GOOD NATURE.

Covetousnesse– Desire of Riches, COVETOUSNESSE: a name used alwayes in signification of blame; because men contending for them, are displeased with one anothers attaining them; though the desire in it selfe, be to be blamed, or allowed, according to the means by which those Riches are sought.

Ambition– Desire of Office, or precedence, AMBITION: a name used also in the worse sense, for the reason before mentioned.

Pusillanimity– Desire of things that conduce but a little to our ends; And fear of things that are but of little hindrance, PUSILLANIMITY.

Magnanimity– Contempt of little helps, and hindrances, MAGNANIMITY.

Valour– Magnanimity, in danger of Death, or Wounds, VALOUR, FORTITUDE.

Liberality– Magnanimity in the use of Riches, LIBERALITY

Miserablenesse– Pusillanimity, in the same WRETCHEDNESSE, MISERABLENESSE; or PARSIMONY; as it is liked or disliked.

Kindnesse– Love of Persons for society, KINDNESSE.

Naturall Lust– Love of Persons for Pleasing the sense onely, NATURAL LUST.

Luxury– Love of the same, acquired from Rumination, that is Imagination of Pleasure past, LUXURY.

The Passion Of Love; Jealousie– Love of one singularly, with desire to be singularly beloved, THE PASSION OF LOVE. The same, with fear that the love is not mutuall,

JEALOUSIE.

Revengefulnesse– Desire, by doing hurt to another, to make him condemn some fact of his own, REVENGEFULNESSE.

Curiosity– Desire, to know why, and how, CURIOSITY; such as is in no living creature but Man; so that Man is distinguished, not onely by his Reason; but also by this singular Passion from other Animals; in whom the appetite of food, and other pleasures of Sense, by praedominance, take away the care of knowing causes; which is a Lust of the mind, that by a perseverance of delight in the continuall and indefatigable generation of Knowledge, exceedeth the short vehemence of any carnall Pleasure.

Religion Superstition; True Religion– Feare of power invisible, feigned by the mind, or imagined from tales publiquely allowed, RELIGION; not allowed, superstition. And when the power imagined is truly such as we imagine, TRUE RELIGION.

Panique Terrour– Feare, without the

apprehension of why, or what, PANIQUE TERROR; called so from the fables that make Pan the author of them; whereas in truth there is always in him that so feareth, first, some apprehension of the cause, though the rest run away by example; every one supposing his fellow to know why. And therefore this Passion happens to none but in a throng, or multitude of people.

Admiration– Joy, from apprehension of novelty, ADMIRATION; proper to man, because it excites the appetite of knowing the cause.

Glory Vaine-glory– Joy, arising from imagination of a man's own power and ability, is that exultation of the mind which is called GLORYING: which, if grounded upon the experience of his own former actions, is the same with Confidence: but if grounded on the flattery of others, or onely supposed by himselfe, for delight in the consequences of it, is called VAINE-GLORY: which name is properly given; because a well-grounded

Confidence begetteth attempt; whereas the supposing of power does not, and is therefore rightly called Vaine.

Dejection– Griefe, from opinion of want of power, is called dejection of mind.

The Vaine-glory which consisteth in the feigning or supposing of abilities in ourselves, which we know are not, is most incident to young men, and nourished by the Histories or Fictions of Gallant Persons; and is corrected often times by Age, and Employment.

Sudden Glory Laughter–Sudden glory, is the passion which maketh those Grimaces called LAUGHTER; and is caused either by some sudden act of their own, that pleaseth them; or by the apprehension of some deformed thing in another, by comparison whereof they suddenly applaud themselves. And it is incident most to them, that are conscious of the fewest abilities in themselves; who are forced to keep themselves in their own favour, by observing the imperfections of other men. And therefore much Laughter at the defects of others is a signe of Pusillanimity. For of great minds, one of the proper workes is, to help and free others from scorn; and compare themselves onely with the most able.

Sudden Dejection Weeping– On the contrary, Sudden Dejection is the passion that causeth WEEPING; and is caused by such accidents, as suddenly take away some vehement hope, or some prop of their power: and they are most subject to it, that rely principally on helps externall, such as are Women, and Children. Therefore, some Weep for the loss of Friends; Others for their unkindnesse; others for the sudden stop made to their thoughts of revenge, by Reconciliation. But in all cases, both Laughter and Weeping, are sudden motions; Custome taking them both away. For no man Laughs at old jests; or Weeps for an old calamity.

Shame Blushing– Griefe, for the discovery of some defect of ability is SHAME, or the passion that discovereth itself in BLUSHING;

and consisteth in the apprehension of some thing dishonourable; and in young men, is a signe of the love of good reputation; and commendable: in old men it is a signe of the same; but because it comes too late, not commendable.

Impudence– The Contempt of good reputation is called IMPUDENCE.

Pitty– Griefe, for the calamity of another is PITTY; and ariseth from the imagination that the like calamity may befall himselfe; and therefore is called also COMPASSION, and in the phrase of this present time a FELLOW-FEELING: and therefore for Calamity arriving from great wickedness, the best men have the least Pitty; and for the same Calamity, those have least Pitty, that think themselves least obnoxious to the same.

Cruelty– Contempt, or little sense of the calamity of others, is that which men call CRUELTY; proceeding from Security of their own fortune. For, that any man should take pleasure in other mens' great harmes, without other end of his own, I do not conceive it possible.

Emulation Envy– Griefe, for the success of a Competitor in wealth, honour, or other good, if it be joyned with Endeavour to enforce our own abilities to equal or exceed him, is called EMULATION: but joyned with Endeavour to supplant or hinder a Competitor, ENVIE.

Deliberation– When in the mind of man, Appetites and Aversions, Hopes and Feares, concerning one and the same thing, arise alternately; and divers good and evill consequences of the doing, or omitting the thing propounded, come successively into our thoughts; so that sometimes we have an Appetite to it, sometimes an Aversion from it; sometimes Hope to be able to do it; sometimes Despaire, or Feare to attempt it; the whole sum of Desires, Aversions, Hopes and Feares, continued till the thing be either done, or thought impossible, is that we call DELIBERATION.

Therefore of things past, there is no Deliberation; because manifestly impossible to be changed: nor of things known to be impossible, or thought so; because men know, or think such Deliberation vaine. But of things impossible, which we think possible, we may Deliberate; not knowing it is in vain. And it is called DELIBERATION; because it is a putting an end to the Liberty we had of doing, or omitting, according to our own Appetite, or Aversion.

This alternate succession of Appetites, Aversions, Hopes and Feares is no less in other living Creatures than in Man; and therefore Beasts also Deliberate.

Every Deliberation is then sayd to End when that whereof they Deliberate, is either done, or thought impossible; because till then wee retain the liberty of doing, or omitting, according to our Appetite, or Aversion.

THE WILL

In Deliberation, the last Appetite, or Aversion, immediately adhaering to the action, or to the omission thereof, is that wee call the WILL; the Act, (not the faculty,) of Willing. And Beasts that have Deliberation must necessarily also have Will. The Definition of the Will, given commonly by the Schooles, that it is a Rationall Appetite, is not good. For if it were, then could there be no Voluntary Act against Reason. For a Voluntary Act is that, which proceedeth from the Will, and no other. But if in stead of a Rationall Appetite, we shall say an Appetite resulting from a precedent Deliberation, then the Definition is the same that I have given here. Will, therefore, Is The Last Appetite In Deliberating. And though we say in common Discourse, a man had a Will once to do a thing, that neverthelesse he forbore to do; yet that is properly but an Inclination, which makes no Action

Voluntary; because the action depends not of it, but of the last Inclination, or Appetite. For if the intervenient Appetites make any action Voluntary, then by the same reason all intervenient Aversions should make the same action Involuntary; and so one and the same action should be both Voluntary & Involuntary.

By this it is manifest, that not onely actions that have their beginning from Covetousness, Ambition, Lust, or other Appetites to the thing propounded; but also those that have their beginning from Aversion, or Feare of those consequences that follow the omission, are Voluntary Actions.

FORMES OF SPEECH, IN PASSION

The formes of Speech by which the Passions are expressed, are partly the same, and partly different from those, by which we express our

Thoughts. And first generally all Passions may be expressed Indicatively; as, I Love, I Feare, I Joy, I Deliberate, I Will, I Command: but some of them have particular expressions by themselves, which nevertheless are not affirmations, unless it be when they serve to make other inferences, besides that of the Passion they proceed from. Deliberation is expressed Subjunctively; which is a speech proper to signifie suppositions, with their consequences; as, If This Be Done, Then This Will Follow; and differs not from the language of Reasoning, save that Reasoning is in generall words, but Deliberation for the most part is of Particulars. The language of Desire, and Aversion, is Imperative; as, Do This, Forbear That; which when the party is obliged to do, or forbear, is Command; otherwise Prayer; or els Counsell. The language of Vaine-Glory, of Indignation, Pitty and Revengefulness, Optative: but of the Desire to know, there is a peculiar expression called Interrogative; as, What Is

It, When Shall It, How Is It Done, and Why So? Other language of the Passions I find none: for Cursing, Swearing, Reviling, and the like, do not signifie as Speech; but as the actions of a tongue accustomed.

These forms of Speech, I say, are expressions, or voluntary significations of our Passions: but certain signes they be not; because they may be used arbitrarily, whether they that use them, have such Passions or not. The best signes of Passions present, are either in the countenance, motions of the body, actions, and ends, or aims, which we otherwise know the man to have.

GOOD AND EVILL APPARENT

And because in Deliberation the Appetites and Aversions are raised by foresight of the good and evill consequences, and sequels of the action whereof we Deliberate; the good or evill effect thereof dependeth on the foresight of a long chain of consequences, of which very seldome any man is able to see to the end. But for so far as a man seeth, if the Good in those consequences be greater than the evill, the whole chain is that which Writers call Apparent or Seeming Good. And contrarily, when the evill exceedeth the good, the whole is Apparent or Seeming Evill: so that he who hath by Experience, or Reason, the greatest and surest prospect of Consequences, Deliberates best himself; and is able, when he will, to give the best counsel unto others.

FELICITY

Continual Successe in obtaining those things which a man from time to time desireth, that is to say, continual prospering, is that men call FELICITY; I mean the Felicity of this life. For there is no such thing as perpetual Tranquillity of mind, while we live here; because Life itself is but Motion, and can never be without Desire, nor without Feare, no more than without Sense. What kind of Felicity God hath ordained to them that devoutly honour him, a man shall no sooner know, than enjoy; being joys, that now are as incomprehensible, as the word of School-men, Beatifical Vision, is unintelligible.

PRAISE MAGNIFICATION

The form of speech whereby men signifie their opinion of the Goodnesse of anything is PRAISE. That whereby they signifie the power and greatness of anything is MAGNIFYING. And that whereby they signifie the opinion they have of a man's felicity is by the Greeks called Makarismos, for which we have no name in our tongue. And thus much is sufficient for the present purpose to have been said of the passions.

CHAPTER SEVEN

Of the Ends or Resolutions of Discourse

OF ALL DISCOURSE, governed by desire of Knowledge, there is at last an End, either by attaining, or by giving over. And in the chain of Discourse, wheresoever it be interrupted, there is an End for that time.

JUDGEMENT, OR SENTENCE FINAL; DOUBT

If the Discourse be meerly Mentall, it consisteth of thoughts that the thing will be, and will not be; or that it has been, and has not been, alternately. So that wheresoever you break off the chayn of a mans Discourse, you leave him in a Praesumption of It Will Be, or, It Will Not Be; or it Has Been, or, Has Not Been. All which is Opinion. And that which is alternate Appetite, in Deliberating concerning Good and Evil, the same is alternate Opinion in the Enquiry of the truth of Past, and Future. And as the last Appetite in Deliberation is called the Will, so the last Opinion in search of the truth of Past, and Future, is called the JUDGEMENT, or Resolute and Final Sentence of him that Discourseth. And as the whole chain of Appetites alternate, in the question of Good or Bad is called Deliberation; so the whole chain of Opinions alternate, in the question of True, or False is called DOUBT.

No Discourse whatsoever, can End in absolute knowledge of Fact, past, or to come. For, as for the knowledge of Fact, it is originally, Sense; and ever after, Memory. And for the knowledge of consequence, which I have said before is called Science, it is not Absolute, but Conditionall. No man can know by Discourse, that this, or that, is, has been, or will be; which is to know absolutely: but onely, that if This be, That is; if This has been, That has been; if This shall be, That shall be: which is to know conditionally; and that not the consequence of one thing to another; but of one name of a thing, to another name of the same thing.

SCIENCE OPINION CONSCIENCE

And therefore, when the Discourse is put into Speech, and begins with the Definitions of Words, and proceeds by Connexion of the same into general Affirmations, and of these again into Syllogismes, the end or last sum is called the Conclusion; and the thought of the mind by it signified is that conditional Knowledge, or Knowledge of the consequence of words, which is commonly called Science. But if the first ground of such Discourse be not Definitions, or if the Definitions be not rightly joyned together into Syllogismes, then the End or Conclusion is again OPINION, namely of the truth of somewhat said, though sometimes in absurd and senslesse words, without possibility of being understood. When two, or more men, know of one and the same fact, they are said to be CONSCIOUS of it one to another; which is as much as to know it together. And because such are fittest witnesses of the facts of one another, or of a third, it was, and ever will be reputed a very Evill act, for any man to speak against his Conscience; or to corrupt or force another so to do: Insomuch that the plea of Conscience, has been always hearkened unto very diligently in all times. Afterwards, men made use of the same word metaphorically, for the knowledge of their own secret facts, and secret thoughts; and therefore it is Rhetorically said that the Conscience is a thousand witnesses. And last of all, men, vehemently in love with their own new opinions, (though never so absurd,) and obstinately bent to maintain them, gave those their opinions also that reverenced name of Conscience, as if they would have it seem unlawful, to change or speak against them; and so pretend to know they are true, when they know at most but that they think so.

BELIEFE FAITH

When a mans Discourse beginneth not at Definitions, it beginneth either at some other contemplation of his own, and then it is still called Opinion; Or it beginneth at some saying of another, of whose ability to know the truth, and of whose honesty in not deceiving, he doubteth not; and then the Discourse is not so much concerning the Thing, as the Person; And the Resolution is called BELEEFE, and FAITH: Faith, In the man; Beleefe, both Of the man, and Of the truth of what he sayes. So then in Beleefe are two opinions; one of the saying of the man; the other of his vertue. To Have Faith In, or Trust To, or Beleeve A Man, signifie the same thing; namely, an opinion of the veracity of the man: But to Beleeve What Is Said, signifieth onely an opinion of the truth of the saying. But wee are to observe that this Phrase, I Beleeve In; as also the Latine, Credo In; and the Greek, Pisteno Eis, are never used but in the writings of Divines. In stead of them, in other writings are put, I Beleeve Him; I Have Faith In Him; I Rely On Him: and in Latin, Credo Illi; Fido Illi: and in Greek, Pisteno Anto: and that this singularity of the Ecclesiastical use of the word hath raised many disputes about the right object of the Christian Faith.

But by Beleeving In, as it is in the Creed, is meant, not trust in the Person; but Confession and acknowledgement of the Doctrine. For not onely Christians, but all manner of men do so believe in God, as to hold all for truth they heare him say, whether they understand it, or not; which is all the Faith and trust can possibly be had in any person whatsoever: But they do not all believe the Doctrine of the Creed.

From whence we may inferre, that when wee believe any saying whatsoever it be, to be true, from arguments taken, not from the thing it selfe, or from the principles of naturall Reason, but from the Authority, and good opinion wee have, of him that hath sayd it; then is the speaker, or person we believe in, or trust in, and whose word we take, the object of our Faith; and the Honour done in Believing, is done to him onely. And consequently, when wee Believe that the Scriptures are the word of God, having no immediate revelation from God himselfe, our Beleefe, Faith, and Trust is in the Church; whose word we take, and acquiesce therein. And they that believe that which a Prophet relates unto them in the name of God, take the word of the Prophet, do honour to him, and in him trust, and believe, touching the truth of what he relateth, whether he be a true, or a false Prophet. And so it is also with all other History. For if I should not believe all that is written By Historians, of the glorious acts of Alexander, or Caesar; I do not think the Ghost of Alexander, or Caesar, had any just cause to be offended; or any body else, but the Historian. If Livy say the Gods made once a Cow speak, and we believe it not; wee distrust not God therein, but Livy. So that it is evident, that whatsoever we believe, upon no other reason, than what is drawn from authority of men onely, and their writings; whether they be sent from God or not, is Faith in men onely.

CHAPTER EIGHT

Of the Vertues Commonly Called Intellectual; and their Contrary Defects

INTELLECTUALL VERTUE DEFINED

VERTUE GENERALLY, in all sorts of subjects, is somewhat that is valued for eminence; and consisteth in comparison.

For if all things were equally in all men, nothing would be prized. And by Vertues INTELLECTUALL, are always understood such abilityes of the mind, as men praise, value, and desire should be in themselves; and go commonly under the name of a Good Witte; though the same word Witte, be used also, to distinguish one certain ability from the rest.

WIT, NATURALL, OR ACQUIRED

These Vertues are of two sorts; Naturall, and Acquired. By Naturall, I mean not, that which a man hath from his Birth: for that is nothing else but Sense; wherein men differ so little one from another, and from brute Beasts, as it is not to be reckoned amongst Vertues. But I mean, that Witte, which is gotten by Use onely, and Experience; without Method, Culture, or Instruction. This NATURALL WITTE, consisteth principally in two things; Celerity Of Imagining, (that is, swift succession of one thought to another;) and Steddy Direction to some approved end. On the Contrary a slow Imagination, maketh that Defect, or fault of the mind, which is commonly called DULNESSE, Stupidity, and sometimes by other names that signifie slownesse of motion, or difficulty to be moved.

GOOD WIT, OR FANCY; GOOD JUDGEMENT; DISCRETION

And this difference of quicknesse, is caused by the difference of mens passions; that love and dislike, some one thing, some another: and therefore some mens thoughts run one way, some another: and are held to, and observe differently the things that passe through their imagination. And whereas in his succession of mens thoughts, there is nothing to observe in the things they think on, but either in what they be Like One Another, or in what they be Unlike, or What They Serve For, or How They Serve To Such A Purpose; Those that observe their similitudes, in case they be such as are but rarely observed by others, are sayd to have a Good Wit; by which, in this occasion, is meant a Good Fancy. But they that observe their differences, and dissimilitudes; which is called Distinguishing, and Discerning, and Judging between thing and thing; in case, such discerning be not easie, are said to have a Good Judgement: and particularly in matter of conversation and businesse; wherein, times, places, and persons are to be discerned, this Vertue is called DISCRETION. The former, that is, Fancy, without the help of Judgement, is not commended as a Vertue: but the later which is Judgement, and Discretion, is commended for it selfe, without the help of Fancy. Besides the Discretion of times, places, and persons, necessary to a good Fancy, there is required also an often application of his thoughts to their End; that is to say, to some use to be made of them. This done; he that hath this Vertue, will be easily fitted with similitudes, that will please, not onely by illustration of his discourse, and adorning it with new and apt metaphors; but also, by the rarity or their invention. But without Steddinesse, and Direction to some End, a great Fancy is one kind of Madnesse; such as they have, that entring into any discourse, are snatched from their purpose, by every thing that comes in their thought, into so many, and so long digressions, and parentheses, that they utterly lose themselves: Which kind of folly, I know no particular name for: but the cause of it is, sometimes want of experience; whereby that seemeth to a man new and rare, which doth not so to others: sometimes Pusillanimity; by which that seems great to him, which other men think a trifle: and whatsoever is new, or great, and therefore thought fit to be told, withdrawes a man by degrees from the intended way of his discourse.

In a good Poem, whether it be Epique, or

Dramatique; as also in Sonnets, Epigrams, and other Pieces, both Judgement and Fancy are required: But the Fancy must be more eminent; because they please for the Extravagancy; but ought not to displease by Indiscretion.

In a good History, the Judgement must be eminent; because the goodnesse consisteth, in the Method, in the Truth, and in the Choyse of the actions that are most profitable to be known. Fancy has no place, but onely in adorning the stile.

In Orations of Prayse, and in Invectives, the Fancy is praedominant; because the designe is not truth, but to Honour or Dishonour; which is done by noble, or by vile comparisons. The Judgement does but suggest what circumstances make an action laudable, or culpable.

In Hortatives, and Pleadings, as Truth, or Disguise serveth best to the Designe in hand; so is the Judgement, or the Fancy most required.

In Demonstration, in Councell, and all rigourous search of Truth, Judgement does all; except sometimes the understanding have need to be opened by some apt similitude; and then there is so much use of Fancy. But for Metaphors, they are in this case utterly excluded. For seeing they openly professe deceipt; to admit them into Councell, or Reasoning, were manifest folly.

And in any Discourse whatsoever, if the defect of Discretion be apparent, how extravagant soever the Fancy be, the whole discourse will be taken for a signe of want of wit; and so will it never when the Discretion is manifest, though the Fancy be never so ordinary.

The secret thoughts of a man run over all things, holy, prophane, clean, obscene, grave, and light, without shame, or blame; which verball discourse cannot do, farther than the Judgement shall approve of the Time, Place, and Persons. An Anatomist, or a Physitian may speak, or write his judgement of unclean things; because it is not to please, but profit: but for another man to write his extravagant, and pleasant fancies of the same, is as if a man, from being tumbled into the dirt, should come and present himselfe before good company. And ‘tis the want of Discretion that makes the difference. Again, in profest remissnesse of mind, and familiar company, a man may play with the sounds, and aequivocal significations of words; and that many times with encounters of extraordinary Fancy: but in a Sermon, or in publique, or before persons unknown, or whom we ought to reverence, there is no Gingling of words that will not be accounted folly: and the difference is onely in the want of Discretion. So that where Wit is wanting, it is not Fancy that is wanting, but Discretion. Judgement therefore without Fancy is Wit, but Fancy without Judgement not.

PRUDENCE

When the thoughts of a man, that has a designe in hand, running over a multitude of things, observes how they conduce to that designe; or what designe they may conduce into; if his observations be such as are not easie, or usuall, This wit of his is called PRUDENCE; and dependeth on much Experience, and Memory of the like things, and their consequences heretofore. In which there is not so much difference of Men, as there is in their Fancies and Judgements; Because the Experience of men equall in age, is not much unequall, as to the quantity; but lyes in different occasions; every one having his private designes. To govern well a family, and a kingdome, are not different degrees of Prudence; but different sorts of businesse; no more then to draw a picture in little, or as great, or greater then the life, are different degrees of Art. A plain husband-man is more Prudent in affaires of his own house, then a Privy Counseller in the affaires of another man.

CRAFT

To Prudence, if you adde the use of unjust, or dishonest means, such as usually are prompted to men by Feare, or Want; you have that Crooked Wisdome, which is called CRAFT; which is a signe of Pusillanimity. For Magnanimity is contempt of unjust, or dishonest helps. And that which the Latines Call Versutia, (translated into English, Shifting,) and is a putting off of a present danger or incommodity, by engaging into a greater, as when a man robbs one to pay another, is but a shorter sighted Craft, called Versutia, from Versura, which signifies taking mony at usurie, for the present payment of interest.

ACQUIRED WIT

As for Acquired Wit, (I mean acquired by method and instruction,) there is none but Reason; which is grounded on the right use of Speech; and produceth the Sciences. But of Reason and Science, I have already spoken in the fifth and sixth Chapters.

The causes of this difference of Witts, are in the Passions: and the difference of Passions, proceedeth partly from the different Constitution of the body, and partly from different Education. For if the difference proceeded from the temper of the brain, and the organs of Sense, either exterior or interior, there would be no lesse difference of men in their Sight, Hearing, or other Senses, than in their Fancies, and Discretions. It proceeds therefore from the Passions; which are different, not onely from the difference of mens complexions; but also from their difference of customes, and education.

The Passions that most of all cause the differences of Wit, are principally, the more or lesse Desire of Power, of Riches, of Knowledge, and of Honour. All which may be reduced to the first, that is Desire of Power. For Riches, Knowledge and Honour are but severall sorts of Power.

GIDDINESSE MADNESSE

And therefore, a man who has no great Passion for any of these things; but is as men terme it indifferent; though he may be so farre a good man, as to be free from giving offence; yet he cannot possibly have either a great Fancy, or much Judgement. For the Thoughts, are to the Desires, as Scouts, and Spies, to range abroad, and find the way to the things Desired: All Stedinesse of the minds motion, and all quicknesse of the same, proceeding from thence. For as to have no Desire, is to be Dead: so to have weak Passions, is Dulnesse; and to have Passions indifferently for every thing, GIDDINESSE, and Distraction; and to have stronger, and more vehement Passions for any thing, than is ordinarily seen in others, is that which men call MADNESSE.

Whereof there be almost as many kinds, as of the Passions themselves. Sometimes the extraordinary and extravagant Passion, proceedeth from the evill constitution of the organs of the Body, or harme done them; and sometimes the hurt, and indisposition of the Organs, is caused by the vehemence, or long continuance of the Passion. But in both cases the Madnesse is of one and the same nature.

The Passion, whose violence, or continuance maketh Madnesse, is either great Vaine-Glory; which is commonly called Pride, and Selfe-Conceipt; or great Dejection of mind.

RAGE

Pride, subjecteth a man to Anger, the excesse whereof, is the Madnesse called RAGE, and FURY. And thus it comes to passe that excessive desire of Revenge, when it becomes habituall, hurteth the organs, and becomes Rage: That excessive love, with jealousie, becomes also Rage: Excessive opinion of a mans own selfe, for divine inspiration, for wisdome, learning, forme, and the like, becomes Distraction, and Giddinesse: the same, joyned with Envy, Rage: Vehement opinion of the truth of any thing, contradicted by others, Rage.

MELANCHOLY

Dejection, subjects a man to causelesse fears; which is a Madnesse commonly called MELANCHOLY, apparent also in divers manners; as in haunting of solitudes, and graves; in superstitious behaviour; and in fearing some one, some another particular thing. In summe, all Passions that produce strange and unusuall behaviour, are called by the generall name of Madnesse. But of the severall kinds of Madnesse, he that would take the paines, might enrowle a legion. And if the Excesses be madnesse, there is no doubt but the Passions themselves, when they tend to Evill, are degrees of the same.

(For example,) Though the effect of folly, in them that are possessed of an opinion of being inspired, be not visible alwayes in one man, by any very extravagant action, that proceedeth from such Passion; yet when many of them conspire together, the Rage of the whole multitude is visible enough. For what argument of Madnesse can there be greater, than to clamour, strike, and throw stones at our best friends? Yet this is somewhat lesse than such a multitude will do. For they will clamour, fight against, and destroy those, by whom all their lifetime before, they have been protected, and secured from injury. And if this be Madnesse in the multitude, it is the same in every particular man. For as in the middest of the sea, though a man perceive no sound of that part of the water next him; yet he is well assured, that part contributes as much, to the Roaring of the Sea, as any other part, of the same quantity: so also, thought wee perceive no great unquietnesse, in one, or two men; yet we may be well assured, that their singular Passions, are parts of the Seditious roaring of a troubled Nation. And if there were nothing else that bewrayed their madnesse; yet that very arrogating such inspiration to themselves, is argument enough. If some man in Bedlam should entertaine you with sober discourse; and you desire in taking leave, to know what he were, that you might another time requite his civility; and he should tell you, he were God the Father; I think you need expect no extravagant action for argument of his Madnesse.

This opinion of Inspiration, called commonly,

Private Spirit, begins very often, from some lucky finding of an Errour generally held by others; and not knowing, or not remembring, by what conduct of reason, they came to so singular a truth, (as they think it, though it be many times an untruth they light on,) they presently admire themselves; as being in the speciall grace of God Almighty, who hath revealed the same to them supernaturally, by his Spirit.

Again, that Madnesse is nothing else, but too much appearing Passion, may be gathered out of the effects of Wine, which are the same with those of the evill disposition of the organs. For the variety of behaviour in men that have drunk too much, is the same with that of Mad-men: some of them Raging, others Loving, others laughing, all extravagantly, but according to their severall domineering Passions: For the effect of the wine, does but remove Dissimulation; and take from them the sight of the deformity of their Passions. For, (I believe) the most sober men, when they walk alone without care and employment of the mind, would be unwilling the vanity and Extravagance of their thoughts at that time should be publiquely seen: which is a confession, that Passions unguided, are for the most part meere Madnesse.

The opinions of the world, both in antient and later ages, concerning the cause of madnesse, have been two. Some, deriving them from the Passions; some, from Daemons, or Spirits, either good, or bad, which they thought might enter into a man, possesse him, and move his organs is such strange, and uncouth manner, as mad-men use to do. The former sort therefore, called such men, Mad-men: but the Later, called them sometimes Daemoniacks, (that is, possessed with spirits;) sometimes Energumeni, (that is agitated, or moved with spirits;) and now in Italy they are called not onely Pazzi, Mad-men; but also Spiritati, men possest.

There was once a great conflux of people

in Abdera, a City of the Greeks, at the acting of the Tragedy of Andromeda, upon an extream hot day: whereupon, a great many of the spectators falling into Fevers, had this accident from the heat, and from The Tragedy together, that they did nothing but pronounce Iambiques, with the names of Perseus and Andromeda; which together with the Fever, was cured, by the comming on of Winter: And this madnesse was thought to proceed from the Passion imprinted by the Tragedy. Likewise there raigned a fit of madnesse in another Graecian city, which seized onely the young Maidens; and caused many of them to hang themselves. This was by most then thought an act of the Divel. But one that suspected, that contempt of life in them, might proceed from some Passion of the mind, and supposing they did not contemne also their honour, gave counsell to the Magistrates, to strip such as so hang'd themselves, and let them hang out naked. This the story sayes cured that madnesse. But on the other side, the same Graecians, did often ascribe madnesse, to the operation of the Eumenides, or Furyes; and sometimes of Ceres, Phoebus, and other Gods: so much did men attribute to Phantasmes, as to think them aereal living bodies; and generally to call them Spirits. And as the Romans in this, held the same opinion with the Greeks: so also did the Jewes; For they calle mad-men Prophets, or (according as they thought the spirits good or bad) Daemoniacks; and some of them called both Prophets, and Daemoniacks, mad-men; and some called the same man both Daemoniack, and mad-man. But for the Gentiles, 'tis no wonder; because Diseases, and Health; Vices, and Vertues; and many naturall accidents, were with them termed, and worshipped as Daemons. So that a man was to understand by Daemon, as well (sometimes) an Ague, as a Divell. But for the Jewes to have such opinion, is somewhat strange. For neither Moses, nor Abraham pretended to Prophecy by possession of a Spirit; but from the voyce of God; or by a Vision or Dream: Nor is there any thing in his Law, Morall, or Ceremoniall, by which they were taught, there was any such Enthusiasme; or any Possession. When God is sayd, (Numb. 11. 25.) to take from the Spirit that was in Moses, and give it to the 70. Elders, the Spirit of God (taking it for the substance of God) is not divided. The Scriptures by the Spirit of God in man, mean a mans spirit, enclined to Godlinesse. And where it is said (Exod. 28. 3.) "Whom I have filled with the Spirit of wisdome to make garments for Aaron," is not meant a spirit put into them, that can make garments; but the wisdome of their own spirits in that kind of work. In the like sense, the spirit of man, when it produceth unclean actions, is ordinarily called an unclean spirit; and so other spirits, though not alwayes, yet as often as the vertue or vice so stiled, is extraordinary, and Eminent. Neither did the other Prophets of the old Testament pretend Enthusiasme; or, that God spake in them; but to them by Voyce, Vision, or Dream; and the Burthen Of The Lord was not Possession, but Command. How then could the Jewes fall into this opinion of possession? I can imagine no reason, but that which is common to all men; namely, the want of curiosity to search naturall causes; and their placing Felicity, in the acquisition of the grosse pleasures of the Senses, and the things that most immediately conduce thereto. For they that see any strange, and unusuall ability, or defect in a mans mind; unlesse they see withall, from what cause it may probably proceed, can hardly think it naturall; and if not naturall, they must needs thinke it supernaturall; and then what can it be, but that either God, or the Divell is in him? And hence it came to passe, when our Saviour (Mark 3.21.) was compassed about with the multitude, those of the house doubted he was mad, and went out to hold him: but the Scribes said he had Belzebub, and that was it, by which he cast out divels; as if the greater mad-man had awed the lesser. And that (John 10. 20.) some said, "He hath a Divell, and is mad;" whereas others holding him for a Prophet, sayd, "These are not the words of one that hath a Divell." So in the old Testament he that came to anoynt Jehu, (2 Kings 9.11.) was a Prophet; but some of the company asked Jehu, "What came that mad-man for?" So that in summe, it is manifest, that whosoever behaved himselfe in extraordinary manner, was thought by the Jewes to be possessed either with a good, or evill spirit; except by the Sadduces, who erred so farre on the other hand, as not to believe there were at all any spirits, (which is very neere to direct Atheisme;) and thereby perhaps the more provoked others, to terme such men Daemoniacks, rather than mad-men.

But why then does our Saviour proceed in the curing of them, as if they were possest;

and not as if they were mad. To which I can give no other kind of answer, but that which is given to those that urge the Scripture in like manner against the opinion of the motion of the Earth. The Scripture was written to shew unto men the kingdome of God; and to prepare their mindes to become his obedient subjects; leaving the world, and the Philosophy thereof, to the disputation of men, for the exercising of their naturall Reason. Whether the Earths, or Suns motion make the day, and night; or whether the Exorbitant actions of men, proceed from Passion, or from the Divell, (so we worship him not) it is all one, as to our obedience, and subjection to God Almighty; which is the thing for which the Scripture was written. As for that our Saviour speaketh to the disease, as to a person; it is the usuall phrase of all that cure by words onely, as Christ did, (and Inchanters pretend to do, whether they speak to a Divel or not.) For is not Christ also said (Math. 8.26.) to have rebuked the winds? Is not he said also (Luk. 4. 39.) to rebuke a Fever? Yet this does not argue that a Fever is a Divel. And whereas many of these Divels are said to confesse Christ; it is not necessary to interpret those places otherwise, than that those mad-men confessed him. And whereas our Saviour (Math. 12. 43.) speaketh of an unclean Spirit, that having gone out of a man, wandreth through dry places, seeking rest, and finding none; and returning into the same man, with seven other spirits worse than himselfe; It is manifestly a Parable, alluding to a man, that after a little endeavour to quit his lusts, is vanquished by the strength of them; and becomes seven times worse than he was. So that I see nothing at all in the Scripture, that requireth a beliefe, that Daemoniacks were any other thing but Mad-men.

INSIGNIFICANT SPEECH

There is yet another fault in the Discourses

of some men; which may also be numbred amongst the sorts of Madnesse; namely, that abuse of words, whereof I have spoken before in the fifth chapter, by the Name of Absurdity. And that is, when men speak such words, as put together, have in them no signification at all; but are fallen upon by some, through misunderstanding of the words they have received, and repeat by rote; by others, from intention to deceive by obscurity. And this is incident to none but those, that converse in questions of matters incomprehensible, as the Schoole-men; or in questions of abstruse Philosophy. The common sort of men seldome speak Insignificantly, and are therefore, by those other Egregious persons counted Idiots. But to be assured their words are without any thing correspondent to them in the mind, there would need some Examples; which if any man require, let him take a Schoole-man into his hands, and see if he can translate any one chapter concerning any difficult point; as the Trinity; the Deity; the nature of Christ; Transubstantiation; Free-will. &c. into any of the moderne tongues, so as to make the same intelligible; or into any tolerable Latine, such as they were acquainted withall, that lived when the Latine tongue was Vulgar. What is the meaning of these words. "The first cause does not necessarily inflow any thing into the second, by force of the Essential subordination of the second causes, by which it may help it to worke?" They are the Translation of the Title of the sixth chapter of Suarez first Booke, Of The Concourse, Motion, And Help Of God. When men write whole volumes of such stuffe, are they not Mad, or intend to make others so? And particularly, in the question of Transubstantiation; where after certain words spoken, they that say, the White-nesse, Round-nesse, Magni-tude, Quali-ty, Corruptibili-ty, all which are incorporeall, &c. go out of the Wafer, into the Body of our blessed Saviour, do they not make those Nesses, Tudes and Ties, to be so many spirits possessing his body? For by Spirits, they mean alwayes things, that being incorporeall, are neverthelesse moveable from one place to another. So that this kind of Absurdity, may rightly be numbred amongst the many sorts of Madnesse; and all the time that guided by clear Thoughts of their worldly lust, they forbear disputing, or writing thus, but Lucide Intervals. And thus much of the Vertues and Defects Intellectuall.

CHAPTER NINE

Of the Severall Subjects of Knowledge

THERE ARE OF KNOWLEDGE two kinds; whereof one is Knowledge Of Fact: the other Knowledge Of The Consequence Of One Affirmation To Another. The former is nothing else, but Sense and Memory, and is Absolute Knowledge; as when we see a Fact doing, or remember it done: And this is the Knowledge required in a Witnesse. The later is called Science; and is Conditionall; as when we know, that, If The Figure Showne Be A Circle, Then Any Straight Line Through The Centre Shall Divide It Into Two Equall Parts. And this is the Knowledge required in a Philosopher; that is to say, of him that pretends to Reasoning.

The Register of Knowledge Of Fact is called History. Whereof there be two sorts: one called Naturall History; which is the History of such Facts, or Effects of Nature, as have no Dependance on Mans Will; Such as are the Histories of Metals, Plants, Animals, Regions, and the like. The other, is Civill History; which is the History of the Voluntary Actions of men in Commonwealths.

The Registers of Science, are such Books as contain the Demonstrations of Consequences of one Affirmation, to another; and are commonly called Books of Philosophy; whereof the sorts are many, according to the diversity of the Matter; And may be divided in such manner as I have divided them in the following Table.

- **I. Science, that is, Knowledge of Consequences; which is called also PHILOSOPHY**
  - **A. Consequences from Accidents of Bodies Naturall; which is called NATURALL PHILOSOPHY**
    - **1. Consequences from the Accidents common to all Bodies Naturall; which are Quantity, and Motion.**
      - **a. Consequences from Quantity, and Motion Indeterminate; which, being the Principles or first foundation of Philosophy, is called Philosophia Prima PHILOSOPHIA PRIMA**
      - **b. Consequences from Motion, and Quantity Determined**
        - **1) Consequences from**

Quantity, and Motion Determined

- a) **By Figure, By Number**
  - 1] **Mathematiques, GEOMETRY ARITHMETIQUE**

2) **Consequences from the Motion, and Quantity of Bodies in Speciall**

- a) **Consequences from the Motion, and Quantity of the great parts of the World, as the Earth and Stars,**
  - 1] **Cosmography ASTRONOMY GEOGRAPHY**
- b) **Consequences from the Motion of Speciall kinds, and Figures of Body,**
  - 1] **Mechaniques, Doctrine of**

Weight Science of ENGINEERS ARCHITECTURE NAVIGATION

2. **PHYSIQUES, or Consequences from Qualities**
   a. **Consequences from the Qualities of Bodies Transient, such as sometimes appear, sometimes vanish METEOROLOGY**
   b. **Consequences from the Qualities of Bodies Permanent**
      1) **Consequences from the Qualities of the Starres**
         a) **Consequences from the Light of the Starres. Out of this, and the Motion of the Sunne, is made the Science of**

SCIOGRAPHY

- b) **Consequences from the Influence of the Starres, ASTROLOGY**

2) **Consequences of the Qualities from Liquid Bodies that fill the space between the Starres; such as are the Ayre, or substance aetherial.**
3) **Consequences from Qualities of Bodies Terrestrial**
   - a) **Consequences from parts of the Earth that are without Sense,**
     - 1] **Consequences from Qualities of Minerals, as Stones, Metals, &c.**
     - 2] **Consequences from the Qualities of Vegetables**

b) Consequences from Qualities of Animals

1] Consequences from Qualities of Animals in Generall

a] Consequences from Vision, OPTIQUES

b] Consequences from Sounds, MUSIQUE

c] Consequences from the rest of the senses

2] Consequences from Qualities of Men in Speciall

a] Consequences from Passions of Men, ETHIQUES

b] Consequences from Speech,

i) In Magnifying, Vilifying, etc. POETRY

ii) In Persuading, RHETORIQUE

iii) In Reasoning, LOGIQUE

iv) In Contracting, The Science of JUST and UNJUST

B. Consequences from the Accidents of Politique Bodies; which is called POLITIQUES, and CIVILL PHILOSOPHY

1. Of Consequences from the Institution of COMMON-WEALTHS, to the Rights, and Duties of the Body Politique, or Soveraign.

2. Of Consequences from the same, to the Duty and Right of the Subjects.

CHAPTER TEN

Of Power, Worth, Dignity, Honour and Worthiness

POWER

THE POWER OF A MAN, (to take it Universally,) is his present means, to obtain some future apparent Good. And is either Originall, or Instrumentall.

Naturall Power, is the eminence of the Faculties of Body, or Mind: as extraordinary

Strength, Forme, Prudence, Arts, Eloquence, Liberality, Nobility. Instrumentall are those Powers, which acquired by these, or by fortune, are means and Instruments to acquire more: as Riches, Reputation, Friends, and the Secret working of God, which men call Good Luck. For the nature of Power, is in this point, like to Fame, increasing as it proceeds; or like the motion of heavy bodies, which the further they go, make still the more hast.

The Greatest of humane Powers, is that which is compounded of the Powers of most men, united by consent, in one person, Naturall, or civill, that has the use of all their Powers depending on his will; such as is the Power of a Common-wealth: or depending on the wills of each particular; such as is the Power of a Faction, or of divers factions leagued. Therefore to have servants, is Power; To have Friends, is Power: for they are strengths united.

Also Riches joyned with liberality, is Power;

because it procureth friends, and servants: Without liberality, not so; because in this case they defend not; but expose men to Envy, as a Prey.

Reputation of power, is Power; because it draweth with it the adhaerance of those that need protection.

So is Reputation of love of a mans Country, (called Popularity,) for the same Reason.

Also, what quality soever maketh a man beloved, or feared of many; or the reputation of such quality, is Power; because it is a means to have the assistance, and service of many.

Good successe is Power; because it maketh reputation of Wisdome, or good fortune; which makes men either feare him, or rely on him.

Affability of men already in power, is encrease of Power; because it gaineth love.

Reputation of Prudence in the conduct of Peace or War, is Power; because to prudent men, we commit the government of our selves, more willingly than to others.

Nobility is Power, not in all places, but onely in those Common-wealths, where it has Priviledges: for in such priviledges consisteth their Power.

Eloquence is Power; because it is seeming Prudence.

Forme is Power; because being a promise of Good, it recommendeth men to the favour of women and strangers.

The Sciences, are small Power; because not eminent; and therefore, not acknowledged in any man; nor are at all, but in a few; and in them, but of a few things. For Science is of that nature, as none can understand it to be, but such as in a good measure have attayned it.

Arts of publique use, as Fortification, making of Engines, and other Instruments of War; because they conferre to Defence, and Victory, are Power; And though the true Mother of them, be Science, namely the Mathematiques; yet, because they are brought into the Light, by the hand of the Artificer, they be esteemed (the Midwife passing with the vulgar for the Mother,) as his issue.

WORTH

The Value, or WORTH of a man, is as of all other things, his Price; that is to say, so much as would be given for the use of his Power: and therefore is not absolute; but a thing dependant on the need and judgement of another. An able conductor of Souldiers, is of great Price in time of War present, or imminent; but in Peace not so. A learned and uncorrupt Judge, is much Worth in time of Peace; but not so much in War. And as in other things, so in men, not the seller, but the buyer determines the Price. For let a man (as most men do,) rate themselves as the highest Value they can; yet their true Value is no more than it is esteemed by others.

The manifestation of the Value we set

on one another, is that which is commonly called Honouring, and Dishonouring. To Value a man at a high rate, is to Honour him; at a low rate, is to Dishonour him. But high, and low, in this case, is to be understood by comparison to the rate that each man setteth on himselfe.

DIGNITY

The publique worth of a man, which is the Value set on him by the Common-wealth, is that which men commonly call DIGNITY. And this Value of him by the Common-wealth, is understood, by offices of Command, Judicature, publike Employment; or by Names and Titles, introduced for distinction of such Value.

TO HONOUR AND DISHONOUR

To pray to another, for ayde of any kind, is to HONOUR; because a signe we have an opinion he has power to help; and the more difficult the ayde is, the more is the Honour.

To obey, is to Honour; because no man obeyes them, whom they think have no power to help, or hurt them. And consequently to disobey, is to Dishonour.

To give great gifts to a man, is to Honour him; because 'tis buying of Protection, and acknowledging of Power. To give little gifts, is to Dishonour; because it is but Almes, and signifies an opinion of the need of small helps. To be sedulous in promoting anothers good; also to flatter, is to Honour; as a signe we seek his protection or ayde. To neglect, is to Dishonour.

To give way, or place to another, in any Commodity, is to Honour; being a confession of greater power. To arrogate, is to Dishonour.

To shew any signe of love, or feare of another, is to Honour; for both to love, and to feare, is to value. To contemne, or lesse to love or feare then he expects, is to Dishonour; for 'tis undervaluing.

To praise, magnifie, or call happy, is to Honour; because nothing but goodnesse, power, and felicity is valued. To revile, mock, or pitty, is to Dishonour.

To speak to another with consideration, to appear before him with decency, and humility, is to Honour him; as signes of fear to offend. To speak to him rashly, to do anything before him obscenely, slovenly, impudently, is to Dishonour.

To believe, to trust, to rely on another, is to Honour him; signe of opinion of his vertue and power. To distrust, or not believe, is to Dishonour.

To hearken to a mans counsell, or discourse of what kind soever, is to Honour; as a signe we think him wise, or eloquent, or witty. To sleep, or go forth, or talk the while, is to Dishonour.

To do those things to another, which he takes for signes of Honour, or which the Law or Custome makes so, is to Honour; because in approving the Honour done by others, he acknowledgeth the power which others acknowledge. To refuse to do them, is to Dishonour.

To agree with in opinion, is to Honour; as being a signe of approving his judgement, and wisdome. To dissent, is Dishonour; and an upbraiding of errour; and (if the dissent be in many things) of folly.

To imitate, is to Honour; for it is vehemently to approve. To imitate ones Enemy, is to Dishonour.

To honour those another honours, is to Honour him; as a signe of approbation of his judgement. To honour his Enemies, is to Dishonour him.

To employ in counsell, or in actions of difficulty, is to Honour; as a signe of opinion of his wisdome, or other power. To deny employment in the same cases, to those that seek it, is to Dishonour.

All these wayes of Honouring, are naturall; and as well within, as without Common-wealths. But in Common-wealths, where he, or they that have the supreme Authority, can make whatsoever they please, to stand for signes of Honour, there be other Honours.

A Soveraigne doth Honour a Subject, with whatsoever Title, or Office, or Employment, or Action, that he himselfe will have taken for a signe of his will to Honour him.

The King of Persia, Honoured Mordecay, when he appointed he should be conducted through the streets in the Kings Garment, upon one of the Kings Horses, with a Crown on his head, and a Prince before him, proclayming, "Thus shall it be done to him that the King will honour." And yet another King of Persia, or the same another time, to one that demanded for some great service, to weare one of the Kings robes, gave him leave so to do; but with his addition, that he should weare it as the Kings foole; and then it was Dishonour. So that of Civill Honour; such as are Magistracy, Offices, Titles; and in some places Coats, and Scutchions painted: and men Honour such as have them, as having so many signes of favour in the Common-wealth; which favour is Power.

Honourable is whatsoever possession, action, or quality, is an argument and signe of Power.

And therefore To be Honoured, loved, or feared of many, is Honourable; as arguments of Power. To be Honoured of few or none, Dishonourable.

Good fortune (if lasting,) Honourable; as a signe of the favour of God. Ill fortune, and losses, Dishonourable. Riches, are Honourable; for they are Power. Poverty, Dishonourable. Magnanimity, Liberality, Hope, Courage, Confidence, are Honourable; for they proceed from the conscience of Power. Pusillanimity, Parsimony, Fear, Diffidence, are Dishonourable.

Timely Resolution, or determination of what a man is to do, is Honourable; as being the contempt of small difficulties, and dangers. And Irresolution, Dishonourable;

as a signe of too much valuing of little impediments, and little advantages: For when a man has weighed things as long as the time permits, and resolves not, the difference of weight is but little; and therefore if he resolve not, he overvalues little things, which is Pusillanimity.

All Actions, and Speeches, that proceed, or seem to proceed from much Experience, Science, Discretion, or Wit, are Honourable; For all these are Powers. Actions, or Words that proceed from Errour, Ignorance, or Folly, Dishonourable.

Gravity, as farre forth as it seems to proceed from a mind employed on some thing else, is Honourable; because employment is a signe of Power. But if it seem to proceed from a purpose to appear grave, it is Dishonourable. For the gravity of the Former, is like the steddinesse of a Ship laden with Merchandise; but of the later, like the steddinesse of a Ship ballasted with Sand, and other trash.

To be Conspicuous, that is to say, to be known, for Wealth, Office, great Actions, or any eminent Good, is Honourable; as a signe of the power for which he is conspicuous. On the contrary, Obscurity, is Dishonourable.

To be descended from conspicuous Parents, is Honourable; because they the more easily attain the aydes, and friends of their Ancestors. On the contrary, to be descended from obscure Parentage, is Dishonourable.

Actions proceeding from Equity, joyned with losse, are Honourable; as signes of Magnanimity: for Magnanimity is a signe of Power. On the contrary, Craft, Shifting, neglect of Equity, is Dishonourable.

Nor does it alter the case of Honour, whether an action (so it be great and difficult, and consequently a signe of much power,) be just or unjust: for Honour consisteth onely in the opinion of Power. Therefore the ancient Heathen did not thinke they Dishonoured, but greatly Honoured the Gods, when they introduced them in their Poems, committing Rapes, Thefts, and other great, but unjust, or unclean acts: In so much as nothing is so much celebrated in Jupiter, as his Adulteries; nor in Mercury, as his Frauds, and Thefts: of whose praises, in a hymne of Homer, the greatest is this, that being born in the morning, he had invented Musique at noon, and before night, stolen away the Cattell of Appollo, from his Herdsmen.

Also amongst men, till there were constituted great Common-wealths, it was thought no dishonour to be a Pyrate, or a High-way Theefe; but rather a lawfull Trade, not onely amongst the Greeks, but also amongst all other Nations; as is manifest by the Histories of antient time. And at this day, in this part of the world, private Duels are, and alwayes will be Honourable, though unlawfull, till such time as there shall be Honour ordained for them that refuse, and Ignominy for them that make the Challenge. For Duels also are many times effects of Courage; and the ground of Courage is alwayes Strength or Skill, which are Power; though for the most part they be effects of rash speaking, and of the fear of Dishonour, in one, or both the Combatants; who engaged by rashnesse, are driven into the Lists to avoyd disgrace.

Scutchions, and coats of Armes haereditary, where they have any eminent Priviledges, are Honourable; otherwise not: for their Power consisteth either in such Priviledges, or in Riches, or some such thing as is equally honoured in other men. This kind of Honour, commonly called Gentry, has been derived from the Antient Germans. For there never was any such thing known, where the German Customes were unknown. Nor is it now any where in use, where the Germans have not inhabited. The antient Greek Commanders, when they went to war, had their Shields painted with such Devises as they pleased; insomuch as an unpainted

Buckler was a signe of Poverty, and of a common Souldier: but they transmitted not the Inheritance of them. The Romans transmitted the Marks of their Families: but they were the Images, not the Devises of their Ancestors. Amongst the people of Asia, Afrique, and America, there is not, nor was ever, any such thing. The Germans onely had that custome; from whom it has been derived into England, France, Spain, and Italy, when in great numbers they either ayded the Romans, or made their own Conquests in these Westerne parts of the world.

For Germany, being antiently, as all other Countries, in their beginnings, divided amongst an infinite number of little Lords, or Masters of Families, that continually had wars one with another; those Masters, or Lords, principally to the end they might, when they were Covered with Arms, be known by their followers; and partly for ornament, both painted their Armor, or their Scutchion, or Coat, with the picture of some Beast, or other thing; and also put some eminent and visible mark upon the Crest of their Helmets. And his ornament both of the Armes, and Crest, descended by inheritance to their Children; to the eldest pure, and to the rest with some note of diversity, such as the Old master, that is to say in Dutch, the Here-alt thought fit. But when many such Families, joyned together, made a greater Monarchy, this duty of the Herealt, to distinguish Scutchions, was made a private Office a part. And the issue of these Lords, is the great and antient Gentry; which for the most part bear living creatures, noted for courage, and rapine; or Castles, Battlements, Belts, Weapons, Bars, Palisadoes, and other notes of War; nothing being then in honour, but vertue military. Afterwards, not onely Kings, but popular Common-wealths, gave divers manners of Scutchions, to such as went forth to the War, or returned from it, for encouragement, or recompence to their service. All which, by an observing Reader, may be found in such ancient Histories, Greek and Latine, as make mention of the German Nation, and Manners, in their times.

TITLES OF HONOUR

Titles of Honour, such as are Duke, Count, Marquis, and Baron, are Honourable; as signifying the value set upon them by the Soveraigne Power of the Common-wealth: Which Titles, were in old time titles of Office, and Command, derived some from the Romans, some from the Germans, and French. Dukes, in Latine Duces, being Generalls in War: Counts, Comites, such as bare the Generall company out of friendship; and were left to govern and defend places conquered, and pacified: Marquises, Marchiones, were Counts that governed the Marches, or bounds of the

Empire. Which titles of Duke, Count, and Marquis, came into the Empire, about the time of Constantine the Great, from the customes of the German Militia. But Baron, seems to have been a Title of the Gaules, and signifies a Great man; such as were the Kings, or Princes men, whom they employed in war about their persons; and seems to be derived from Vir, to Ber, and Bar, that signified the same in the Language of the Gaules, that Vir in Latine; and thence to Bero, and Baro: so that such men were called Berones, and after Barones; and (in Spanish) Varones. But he that would know more particularly the originall of Titles of Honour, may find it, as I have done this, in Mr. Seldens most excellent Treatise of that subject. In processe of time these offices of Honour, by occasion of trouble, and for reasons of good and peacable government, were turned into meer Titles; serving for the most part, to distinguish the precedence, place, and order of subjects in the Common-wealth: and men were made Dukes, Counts, Marquises, and Barons of Places, wherein they had neither possession, nor command: and other Titles also, were devised to the same end.

WORTHINESSE FITNESSE

WORTHINESSE, is a thing different from the worth, or value of a man; and also from his merit, or desert; and consisteth in a particular power, or ability for that, whereof he is said to be worthy: which particular ability, is usually named FITNESSE, or Aptitude.

For he is Worthiest to be a Commander, to be a Judge, or to have any other charge, that is best fitted, with the qualities required to the well discharging of it; and Worthiest of Riches, that has the qualities most requisite for the well using of them: any of which qualities being absent, one may neverthelesse be a Worthy man, and valuable for some thing else. Again, a man may be Worthy of Riches,

Office, and Employment, that neverthelesse, can plead no right to have it before another; and therefore cannot be said to merit or deserve it. For Merit, praesupposeth a right, and that the thing deserved is due by promise: Of which I shall say more hereafter, when I shall speak of Contracts.

CHAPTER ELEVEN

Of the Difference of Manners

WHAT IS HERE MEANT BY MANNERS

BY MANNERS, I mean not here, Decency of behaviour; as how one man should salute another, or how a man should wash his mouth, or pick his teeth before company, and such other points of the Small Morals; But those qualities of man-kind, that concern their living together in Peace, and

Unity. To which end we are to consider, that the Felicity of this life, consisteth not in the repose of a mind satisfied. For there is no such Finis Ultimus, (utmost ayme,) nor Summum Bonum, (greatest good,) as is spoken of in the Books of the old Morall Philosophers. Nor can a man any more live, whose Desires are at an end, than he, whose Senses and Imaginations are at a stand. Felicity is a continuall progresse of the desire, from one object to another; the attaining of the former, being still but the way to the later. The cause whereof is, That the object of mans desire, is not to enjoy once onely, and for one instant of time; but to assure for ever, the way of his future desire. And therefore the voluntary actions, and inclinations of all men, tend, not only to the procuring, but also to the assuring of a contented life; and differ onely in the way: which ariseth partly from the diversity of passions, in divers men; and partly from the difference of the knowledge, or opinion each one has of the causes, which produce the effect desired.

A RESTLESSE DESIRE OF POWER, IN ALL MEN

So that in the first place, I put for a generall inclination of all mankind, a perpetuall and restlesse desire of Power after power, that ceaseth onely in Death. And the cause of this, is not alwayes that a man hopes for a more intensive delight, than he has already attained to; or that he cannot be content with a moderate power: but because he cannot assure the power and means to live well, which he hath present, without the acquisition of more. And from hence it is, that Kings, whose power is greatest, turn their endeavours to the assuring it a home by Lawes, or abroad by Wars: and when that is done, there succeedeth a new desire; in some, of Fame from new Conquest; in others, of ease and sensuall pleasure; in others, of admiration, or being flattered for excellence in some art, or other ability of the mind.

LOVE OF CONTENTION FROM COMPETITION

Competition of Riches, Honour, command, or other power, enclineth to Contention, Enmity, and War: because the way of one Competitor, to the attaining of his desire, is to kill, subdue, supplant, or repell the other. Particularly, competition of praise, enclineth to a reverence of Antiquity. For men contend with the living, not with the dead; to these ascribing more than due, that they may obscure the glory of the other.

CIVIL OBEDIENCE FROM LOVE OF EASE

Desire of Ease, and sensuall Delight,

disposeth men to obey a common Power: because by such Desires, a man doth abandon the protection might be hoped for from his own Industry, and labour.

FROM FEARE OF DEATH OR WOUNDS

Fear of Death, and Wounds, disposeth to the same; and for the same reason. On the contrary, needy men, and hardy, not contented with their present condition; as also, all men that are ambitious of Military command, are enclined to continue the causes of warre; and to stirre up trouble and sedition: for there is no honour Military but by warre; nor any such hope to mend an ill game, as by causing a new shuffle.

AND FROM LOVE OF ARTS

Desire of Knowledge, and Arts of Peace, enclineth men to obey a common Power: For such Desire, containeth a desire of leasure; and consequently protection from some other Power than their own.

LOVE OF VERTUE, FROM LOVE OF PRAISE

Desire of Praise, disposeth to laudable actions, such as please them whose judgement they value; for of these men whom we contemn, we contemn also the Praises. Desire of Fame after death does the same. And though after death, there be no sense of the praise given us on Earth, as being joyes, that are either swallowed up in the unspeakable joyes of Heaven, or extinguished in the extreme torments of Hell: yet is not such Fame vain; because men have a present delight therein, from the foresight of it, and of the benefit that may rebound thereby to their posterity: which though they now see not, yet they imagine; and any thing that is pleasure in the sense, the same also is pleasure in the imagination.

HATE, FROM DIFFICULTY OF REQUITING GREAT BENEFITS

To have received from one, to whom we think our selves equall, greater benefits than there is hope to Requite, disposeth to counterfiet love; but really secret hatred; and puts a man into the estate of a desperate debtor, that in declining the sight of his creditor, tacitely wishes him there, where he might never see him more. For benefits oblige; and obligation is thraldome; which is to ones equall, hateful. But to have received benefits from one, whom we acknowledge our superiour, enclines to love; because the obligation is no new depession: and cheerfull acceptation, (which men call Gratitude,) is such an honour done to the obliger, as is taken generally for retribution. Also to receive benefits, though from an equall, or inferiour, as long as there is hope of requitall, disposeth to love: for in the intention of the receiver, the obligation is of ayd, and service mutuall; from whence proceedeth an Emulation of who shall exceed in benefiting; the most noble and profitable contention possible; wherein the victor is pleased with his victory, and the other revenged by confessing it.

AND FROM CONSCIENCE OF DESERVING TO BE HATED

To have done more hurt to a man, than he can, or is willing to expiate, enclineth the doer to hate the sufferer. For he must expect revenge, or forgivenesse; both which are hatefull.

PROMPTNESSE TO HURT, FROM FEAR

Feare of oppression, disposeth a man to anticipate, or to seek ayd by society: for there is no other way by which a man can secure his life and liberty.

AND FROM DISTRUST OF THEIR OWN WIT

Men that distrust their own subtilty, are in tumult, and sedition, better disposed for victory, than they that suppose themselves wise, or crafty. For these love to consult, the other (fearing to be circumvented,) to strike first. And in sedition, men being alwayes in the procincts of Battell, to hold together, and use all advantages of force, is a better stratagem, than any that can proceed from subtilty of Wit.

VAIN UNDERTAKING FROM VAIN-GLORY

Vain-glorious men, such as without being conscious to themselves of great sufficiency, delight in supposing themselves gallant men, are enclined onely to ostentation; but not to attempt: Because when danger or difficulty appears, they look for nothing but to have their insufficiency discovered.

Vain-glorious men, such as estimate their sufficiency by the flattery of other men, or the fortune of some precedent action, without assured ground of hope from the true knowledge of themselves, are enclined to rash engaging; and in the approach of danger, or difficulty, to retire if they can: because not seeing the way of safety, they will rather hazard their honour, which may be salved with an excuse; than their lives, for which no salve is sufficient.

AMBITION, FROM OPINION OF SUFFICIENCY

Men that have a strong opinion of their own wisdome in matter of government, are disposed to Ambition. Because without publique Employment in counsell or magistracy, the honour of their wisdome is lost. And therefore Eloquent speakers are enclined to Ambition; for Eloquence seemeth wisdome, both to themselves and others

IRRESOLUTION, FROM TOO GREAT VALUING OF SMALL MATTERS

Pusillanimity disposeth men to Irresolution, and consequently to lose the occasions, and fittest opportunities of action. For after men have been in deliberation till the time of action approach, if it be not then manifest what is best to be done, tis a signe, the difference of Motives, the one way and the other, are not great: Therefore not to resolve then, is to lose the occasion by weighing of trifles; which is pusillanimity.

Frugality,(though in poor men a Vertue,) maketh a man unapt to atchieve such actions, as require the strength of many men at once: For it weakeneth their Endeavour, which is to be nourished and kept in vigor by Reward.

Confidence In Others From Ignorance Of The Marks Of Wisdome and Kindnesse Eloquence, with flattery, disposeth men to confide in them that have it; because the former is seeming Wisdome, the later seeming Kindnesse. Adde to them Military reputation, and it disposeth men to adhaere, and subject themselves to those men that have them. The two former, having given them caution against danger from him; the later gives them caution against danger from others.

AND FROM THE IGNORANCE OF NATURALL CAUSES

Want of Science, that is, Ignorance of causes, disposeth, or rather constraineth a man to rely on the advise, and authority of others. For all men whom the truth concernes, if they rely not on their own, must rely on the opinion of some other, whom they think wiser than themselves, and see not why he should deceive them.

AND FROM WANT OF UNDERSTANDING

Ignorance of the signification of words; which is, want of understanding, disposeth men to take on trust, not onely the truth they know not; but also the errors; and which is more, the non-sense of them they trust: For neither Error, nor non-sense, can without a perfect understanding of words, be detected.

From the same it proceedeth, that men give different names, to one and the same thing, from the difference of their own passions: As they that approve a private opinion, call it Opinion; but they that mislike it, Haeresie: and yet haeresie signifies no more than private opinion; but has onely a greater tincture of choler.

From the same also it proceedeth, that men cannot distinguish, without study and great understanding, between one action of many men, and many actions of one multitude; as for example, between the one action of all the Senators of Rome in killing Catiline, and the many actions of a number of Senators in killing Caesar; and therefore are disposed to take for the action of the people, that which is a multitude of actions done by a multitude of men, led perhaps by the perswasion of one.

Adhaerence To Custome, From Ignorance Of The Nature Of Right And Wrong Ignorance of the causes, and originall constitution of Right, Equity, Law, and Justice, disposeth a man to make Custome and Example the rule of his actions; in such manner, as to think that Unjust which it hath been the custome to punish; and that Just, of the impunity and approbation whereof they can produce an Example, or (as the Lawyers which onely use the false measure of Justice barbarously call it) a Precedent; like little children, that have no other rule of good and evill manners, but the correction they receive from their Parents, and Masters; save that children are constant to their rule, whereas men are not so; because grown strong, and stubborn, they appeale from custome to reason, and from reason to custome, as it serves their turn; receding from custome when their interest requires it, and setting themselves against reason, as oft as reason is against them: Which is the cause, that the doctrine of Right and Wrong, is perpetually disputed, both by the Pen and the Sword: whereas the doctrine of Lines, and Figures, is not so; because men care not, in that subject what be truth, as a thing that crosses no mans ambition, profit, or lust. For I doubt not, but if it had been a thing contrary to any mans right of dominion, or to the interest of men that have dominion, That The Three Angles Of

A Triangle Should Be Equall To Two Angles Of A Square; that doctrine should have been, if not disputed, yet by the burning of all books of Geometry, suppressed, as farre as he whom it concerned was able.

Adhaerence To Private Men, From Ignorance Of The Causes Of Peace Ignorance of remote causes, disposeth men to attribute all events, to the causes immediate, and Instrumentall: For these are all the causes they perceive. And hence it comes to passe, that in all places, men that are grieved with payments to the Publique, discharge their anger upon the Publicans, that is to say, Farmers, Collectors, and other Officers of the publique Revenue; and adhaere to such as find fault with the publike Government; and thereby, when they have engaged themselves beyond hope of justification, fall also upon the Supreme Authority, for feare of punishment, or shame of receiving pardon.

CREDULITY FROM IGNORANCE OF NATURE

Ignorance of naturall causes disposeth a man to Credulity, so as to believe many times impossibilities: for such know nothing to the contrary, but that they may be true; being unable to detect the Impossibility. And Credulity, because men love to be hearkened unto in company, disposeth them to lying: so that Ignorance it selfe without Malice, is able to make a man bothe to believe lyes, and tell them; and sometimes also to invent them.

CURIOSITY TO KNOW, FROM CARE OF FUTURE TIME

Anxiety for the future time, disposeth men to enquire into the causes of things: because the knowledge of them, maketh men the better able to order the present to their best advantage.

NATURALL RELIGION, FROM THE SAME

Curiosity, or love of the knowledge of causes, draws a man from consideration of the effect, to seek the cause; and again, the cause of that cause; till of necessity he must come to this thought at last, that there is some cause, whereof there is no former cause, but is eternall; which is it men call God. So that it is impossible to make any profound enquiry into naturall causes, without being enclined thereby to believe there is one God Eternall; though they cannot have any Idea of him in their mind, answerable to his nature. For as a man that is born blind, hearing men talk of warming themselves by the fire, and being brought to warm himself by the same, may easily conceive, and assure himselfe, there is somewhat there, which men call Fire, and is the cause of the heat he feeles; but cannot imagine what it is like; nor have an

Idea of it in his mind, such as they have that see it: so also, by the visible things of this world, and their admirable order, a man may conceive there is a cause of them, which men call God; and yet not have an Idea, or Image of him in his mind.

And they that make little, or no enquiry into the naturall causes of things, yet from the feare that proceeds from the ignorance it selfe, of what it is that hath the power to do them much good or harm, are enclined to suppose, and feign unto themselves, severall kinds of Powers Invisible; and to stand in awe of their own imaginations; and in time of distresse to invoke them; as also in the time of an expected good successe, to give them thanks; making the creatures of their own fancy, their Gods. By which means it hath come to passe, that from the innumerable variety of Fancy, men have created in the world innumerable sorts of Gods. And this Feare of things invisible, is the naturall Seed of that, which every one in himself calleth Religion; and in them that worship, or feare that Power otherwise than they do, Superstition.

And this seed of Religion, having been observed by many; some of those that have observed it, have been enclined thereby to nourish, dresse, and forme it into Lawes; and to adde to it of their own invention, any opinion of the causes of future events, by which they thought they should best be able to govern others, and make unto themselves the greatest use of their Powers.

CHAPTER TWELVE

Of Religion

RELIGION, IN MAN ONELY

SEEING THERE ARE NO SIGNES, nor fruit of Religion, but in Man onely; there is no cause to doubt, but that the seed of Religion, is also onely in Man; and consisteth in some peculiar quality, or at least in some eminent degree thereof, not to be found in other Living creatures.

FIRST, FROM HIS DESIRE OF KNOWING CAUSES

And first, it is peculiar to the nature of Man, to be inquisitive into the Causes of the Events they see, some more, some lesse; but all men so much, as to be curious in the search of the causes of their own good and evill fortune.

FROM THE CONSIDERATION OF THE BEGINNING OF THINGS

Secondly, upon the sight of any thing that hath a Beginning, to think also it had a cause, which determined the same to begin, then when it did, rather than sooner or later.

FROM HIS OBSERVATION OF THE SEQUELL OF THINGS

Thirdly, whereas there is no other Felicity of Beasts, but the enjoying of their quotidian

Food, Ease, and Lusts; as having little, or no foresight of the time to come, for want of observation, and memory of the order, consequence, and dependance of the things they see; Man observeth how one Event hath been produced by another; and remembreth in them Antecedence and Consequence; And when he cannot assure himselfe of the true causes of things, (for the causes of good and evill fortune for the most part are invisible,) he supposes causes of them, either such as his own fancy suggesteth; or trusteth to the Authority of other men, such as he thinks to be his friends, and wiser than himselfe.

The Naturall Cause Of Religion, The Anxiety Of The Time To Come The two first, make Anxiety. For being assured that there be causes of all things that have arrived hitherto, or shall arrive hereafter; it is impossible for a man, who continually endeavoureth to secure himselfe against the evill he feares, and procure the good he desireth, not to be in a perpetuall solicitude of the time to come; So that every man, especially those that are over provident, are in an estate like to that of Prometheus. For as Prometheus, (which interpreted, is, The Prudent Man,) was bound to the hill Caucasus, a place of large prospect, where, an Eagle feeding on his liver, devoured in the day, as much as was repayred in the night: So that man, which looks too far before him, in the care of future time, hath his heart all the day long, gnawed on by feare of death, poverty, or other calamity; and has no repose, nor pause of his anxiety, but in sleep.

WHICH MAKES THEM FEAR THE POWER OF INVISIBLE THINGS

This perpetuall feare, alwayes accompanying mankind in the ignorance of causes, as it were in the Dark, must needs have for object something. And therefore when there is nothing to be seen, there is nothing to accuse, either of their good, or evill fortune, but some Power, or Agent Invisible: In which sense perhaps it was, that some of the old Poets said, that the Gods were at first created by humane Feare: which spoken of the Gods, (that is to say, of the many Gods of the Gentiles) is very true. But the acknowledging of one God Eternall, Infinite, and Omnipotent, may more easily be derived, from the desire men have to know the causes of naturall bodies, and their severall vertues, and operations; than from the feare of what was to befall them in time to come. For he that from any effect hee seeth come to passe, should reason to the next and immediate cause thereof, and from thence to the cause of that cause, and plonge himselfe profoundly in the pursuit of causes; shall at last come to this, that there must be (as even the Heathen Philosophers confessed) one First Mover; that is, a First, and an Eternall cause of all things; which is that which men mean by the name of God: And all this without thought of their fortune; the solicitude whereof, both enclines to fear, and hinders them from the search of the causes of other things; and thereby gives occasion of feigning of as many Gods, as there be men that feigne them.

AND SUPPOSE THEM INCORPOREALL

And for the matter, or substance of the Invisible Agents, so fancyed; they could not by naturall cogitation, fall upon any other conceipt, but that it was the same with that of the Soule of man; and that the Soule of man, was of the same substance, with that which appeareth in a Dream, to one that sleepeth; or in a Looking-glasse, to one that is awake; which, men not knowing that such apparitions are nothing else but creatures of the Fancy, think to be reall, and externall Substances; and therefore call them Ghosts; as the Latines called them Imagines, and Umbrae; and thought them Spirits, that is, thin aereall bodies; and those Invisible Agents, which they feared, to bee like them; save that they appear, and vanish when they please. But the opinion that such Spirits were Incorporeall, or Immateriall, could never enter into the mind of any man by nature; because, though men may put together words of contradictory signification, as Spirit, and Incorporeall; yet they can never have the imagination of any thing answering to them: And therefore, men that by their own meditation, arrive to the acknowledgement of one Infinite, Omnipotent, and Eternall God, choose rather to confesse he is Incomprehensible, and above their understanding; than to define his Nature By Spirit Incorporeall, and then Confesse their definition to be unintelligible: or if they give him such a title, it is not Dogmatically, with intention to make the Divine Nature understood; but Piously, to honour him with attributes, of significations, as remote as they can from the grossenesse of Bodies Visible.

BUT KNOW NOT THE WAY HOW THEY EFFECT ANYTHING

Then, for the way by which they think these Invisible Agents wrought their effects; that is to say, what immediate causes they used, in bringing things to passe, men that know not what it is that we call Causing, (that is, almost all men) have no other rule to guesse by, but by observing, and remembring what they have seen to precede the like effect at some other time, or times before, without seeing between the antecedent and subsequent Event, any dependance or connexion at all: And therefore from the like things past, they expect the like things to come; and hope for good or evill luck, superstitiously, from things that have no part at all in the causing of it: As the Athenians did for their war at Lepanto, demand another Phormio; the Pompeian faction for their warre in Afrique, another Scipio; and others have done in divers other occasions since. In like manner they attribute their fortune to a stander by, to a lucky or unlucky place, to words spoken, especially if the name of God be amongst them; as Charming, and Conjuring (the Leiturgy of Witches;) insomuch as to believe, they have power to turn a stone into bread, bread into a man, or any thing, into any thing.

BUT HONOUR THEM AS THEY HONOUR MEN

Thirdly, for the worship which naturally men exhibite to Powers invisible, it can be no other, but such expressions of their reverence, as they would use towards men; Gifts, Petitions, Thanks, Submission of Body, Considerate Addresses, sober Behaviour, premeditated Words, Swearing (that is, assuring one another of their promises,) by invoking them. Beyond that reason suggesteth nothing; but leaves them either to rest there; or for further ceremonies, to rely on those they believe to be wiser than themselves.

AND ATTRIBUTE TO THEM ALL EXTRAORDINARY EVENTS

Lastly, concerning how these Invisible Powers declare to men the things which shall hereafter come to passe, especially concerning their good or evill fortune in generall, or good or ill successe in any particular undertaking, men are naturally at a stand; save that using to conjecture of the time to come, by the time past, they are very apt, not onely to take casuall things, after one or two encounters, for Prognostiques of the like encounter ever after, but also to believe the like Prognostiques from other men, of whom they have once conceived a good opinion.

FOURE THINGS, NATURALL SEEDS OF RELIGION

And in these foure things, Opinion of Ghosts, Ignorance of second causes, Devotion towards what men fear, and Taking of things Casuall for Prognostiques, consisteth the Naturall seed of Religion; which by reason of the different Fancies, Judgements, and Passions of severall men, hath grown up into ceremonies so different, that those which are used by one man, are for the most part ridiculous to another.

MADE DIFFERENT BY CULTURE

For these seeds have received culture from two sorts of men. One sort have been they, that have nourished, and ordered them, according to their own invention. The other, have done it, by Gods commandement, and direction: but both sorts have done it, with a purpose to make those men that relyed on them, the more apt to Obedience, Lawes, Peace, Charity, and civill Society. So that the Religion of the former sort, is a part of humane Politiques; and teacheth part of the duty which Earthly Kings require of their Subjects. And the Religion of the later sort is Divine Politiques; and containeth Precepts to those that have yeelded themselves subjects in the Kingdome of God. Of the former sort, were all the Founders of Common-wealths, and the Law-givers of the Gentiles: Of the later sort, were Abraham, Moses, and our Blessed Saviour; by whom have been derived unto us the Lawes of the Kingdome of God.

THE ABSURD OPINION OF GENTILISME

And for that part of Religion, which consisteth in opinions concerning the nature of Powers Invisible, there is almost nothing that has a name, that has not been esteemed amongst the Gentiles, in one place or another, a God, or Divell; or by their Poets feigned to be inanimated, inhabited, or possessed by some Spirit or other.

The unformed matter of the World, was a God, by the name of Chaos.

The Heaven, the Ocean, the Planets, the Fire, the Earth, the Winds, were so many Gods.

Men, Women, a Bird, a Crocodile, a Calf, a Dogge, a Snake, an Onion, a Leeke, Deified. Besides, that they filled almost all places, with spirits called Daemons; the plains, with Pan, and Panises, or Satyres; the Woods, with Fawnes, and Nymphs; the Sea, with Tritons, and other Nymphs; every River, and Fountayn, with a Ghost of his name, and with Nymphs; every house, with it Lares, or Familiars; every man, with his Genius; Hell, with Ghosts, and spirituall Officers, as Charon, Cerberus, and the Furies; and in the night time, all places with Larvae, Lemures,

Ghosts of men deceased, and a whole kingdome of Fayries, and Bugbears. They have also ascribed Divinity, and built Temples to meer Accidents, and Qualities; such as are Time, Night, Day, Peace, Concord, Love, Contention, Vertue, Honour, Health, Rust, Fever, and the like; which when they prayed for, or against, they prayed to, as if there were Ghosts of those names hanging over their heads, and letting fall, or withholding that Good, or Evill, for, or against which they prayed. They invoked also their own Wit, by the name of Muses; their own Ignorance, by the name of Fortune; their own Lust, by the name of Cupid; their own Rage, by the name Furies; their own privy members by the name of Priapus; and attributed their pollutions, to Incubi, and Succubae: insomuch as there was nothing, which a Poet could introduce as a person in his Poem, which they did not make either a God, or a Divel.

The same authors of the Religion of the Gentiles, observing the second ground for Religion, which is mens Ignorance of causes; and thereby their aptnesse to attribute their fortune to causes, on which there was no dependence at all apparent, took occasion to obtrude on their ignorance, in stead of second causes, a kind of second and ministeriall Gods; ascribing the cause of Foecundity, to Venus; the cause of Arts, to Apollo; of Subtilty and Craft, to Mercury; of Tempests and stormes, to Aeolus; and of other effects, to other Gods: insomuch as there was amongst the Heathen almost as great variety of Gods, as of businesse.

And to the Worship, which naturally men conceived fit to bee used towards their Gods, namely Oblations, Prayers, Thanks, and the rest formerly named; the same Legislators of the Gentiles have added their Images, both in Picture, and Sculpture; that the more ignorant sort, (that is to say, the most part, or generality of the people,) thinking the Gods for whose representation they were made, were really included, and as it were housed within them, might so much the more stand in feare of them: And endowed them with lands, and houses, and officers, and revenues, set apart from all other humane uses; that is, consecrated, and made holy to those their Idols; as Caverns, Groves, Woods, Mountains, and whole Ilands; and have attributed to them, not onely the shapes, some of Men, some of Beasts, some of Monsters; but also the Faculties, and Passions of men and beasts; as Sense, Speech, Sex, Lust, Generation, (and this not onely by mixing one with another, to propagate the kind of Gods; but also by mixing with men, and women, to beget mongrill Gods, and but inmates of Heaven, as Bacchus, Hercules, and others;) besides, Anger, Revenge, and other passions of living creatures, and the actions proceeding from them, as Fraud, Theft, Adultery, Sodomie, and any vice that may be taken for an effect of Power, or a cause of Pleasure; and all such Vices, as amongst men are taken to be against Law, rather than against Honour.

Lastly, to the Prognostiques of time to come; which are naturally, but Conjectures upon the Experience of time past; and supernaturall, divine Revelation; the same authors of the Religion of the Gentiles, partly upon pretended Experience, partly upon pretended Revelation, have added innumerable other superstitious wayes of Divination; and made men believe they should find their fortunes, sometimes in the ambiguous or senslesse answers of the priests at Delphi, Delos, Ammon, and other famous Oracles; which answers, were made ambiguous by designe, to own the event both wayes; or absurd by the intoxicating vapour of the place, which is very frequent in sulphurous Cavernes: Sometimes in the leaves of the Sibills; of whose Prophecyes (like those perhaps of Nostradamus; for the fragments now extant seem to be the invention of later times) there were some books in reputation in the time of the Roman Republique: Sometimes in the insignificant Speeches of Mad-men, supposed to be possessed with a divine Spirit; which Possession they called Enthusiasme; and these kinds of foretelling events, were accounted Theomancy, or Prophecy; Sometimes in the aspect of the Starres at their Nativity; which was called Horoscopy, and esteemed a part of judiciary Astrology: Sometimes in their own hopes and feares, called Thumomancy, or Presage: Sometimes in the Prediction of Witches, that pretended conference with the dead; which is called Necromancy, Conjuring, and Witchcraft; and is but juggling and confederate knavery: Sometimes in the Casuall flight, or feeding of birds; called Augury: Sometimes in the Entrayles of a sacrificed beast; which was Aruspicina: Sometimes in Dreams: Sometimes in Croaking of Ravens, or chattering of Birds: Sometimes in the Lineaments of the face; which was called Metoposcopy; or by Palmistry in the lines of the hand; in casuall words, called Omina: Sometimes in Monsters, or unusuall accidents; as Ecclipses, Comets, rare Meteors, Earthquakes, Inundations, uncouth Births, and the like, which they called Portenta and Ostenta, because they thought them to portend, or foreshew some great Calamity to come; Sometimes, in meer Lottery, as Crosse and Pile; counting holes in a sive; dipping of Verses in Homer, and Virgil; and innumerable other such vaine conceipts. So easie are men to be drawn to believe any thing, from such men as have gotten credit with them; and can with gentlenesse, and dexterity, take hold of their fear, and ignorance.

The Designes Of The Authors Of The Religion Of The Heathen And therefore the first Founders, and Legislators of Common-wealths amongst the Gentiles, whose ends were only to keep the people in obedience, and peace, have in all places taken care; First, to imprint in their minds a beliefe, that those precepts which they gave concerning Religion, might not be thought to proceed from their own device, but from the dictates of some God, or other Spirit; or else that they themselves were of a higher nature than mere mortalls, that their Lawes might the more easily be received: So Numa Pompilius pretended to receive the Ceremonies he instituted amongst the Romans, from the Nymph Egeria: and the first King and founder of the Kingdome of Peru, pretended himselfe and his wife to be the children of the Sunne: and Mahomet, to set up his new Religion, pretended to have conferences with the Holy Ghost, in forme of a Dove. Secondly, they have had a care, to make it believed, that the same things were displeasing to the Gods, which were forbidden by the Lawes. Thirdly, to prescribe Ceremonies, Supplications, Sacrifices, and Festivalls, by which they were to believe, the anger of the Gods might be appeased; and that ill success in War, great contagions of Sicknesse, Earthquakes, and each mans private Misery, came from the Anger of the Gods; and their Anger from the Neglect of their Worship, or the forgetting, or mistaking some point of the Ceremonies required. And though amongst the antient Romans, men were not forbidden to deny, that which in the Poets is written of the paines, and pleasures after this life; which divers of great authority, and gravity in that state have in their Harangues openly derided; yet that beliefe was alwaies more cherished, than the contrary.

And by these, and such other Institutions, they obtayned in order to their end, (which was the peace of the Commonwealth,) that the common people in their misfortunes, laying the fault on neglect, or errour in their Ceremonies, or on their own disobedience to the lawes, were the lesse apt to mutiny against their Governors. And being entertained with the pomp, and pastime of Festivalls, and publike Gomes, made in honour of the Gods, needed nothing else but bread, to keep them from discontent, murmuring, and commotion against the State. And therefore the Romans, that had conquered the greatest part of the then known World, made no scruple of tollerating any Religion whatsoever in the City of Rome it selfe; unlesse it had somthing in it, that could not consist with their Civill Government; nor do we read, that any Religion was there forbidden, but that of the Jewes; who (being the peculiar Kingdome of God) thought it unlawfull to acknowledge subjection to any mortall King or State whatsoever. And thus you see how the Religion of the Gentiles was a part of their Policy.

The True Religion, And The Lawes Of Gods Kingdome The Same But where God himselfe, by supernaturall Revelation, planted Religion; there he also made to himselfe a peculiar Kingdome; and gave Lawes, not only of behaviour towards himselfe; but also towards one another; and thereby in the Kingdome of God, the Policy, and lawes Civill, are a part of Religion; and therefore the distinction of Temporall, and Spirituall Domination, hath there no place. It is true, that God is King of all the Earth: Yet may he be King of a peculiar, and chosen Nation. For there is no more incongruity therein, than that he that hath the generall command of the whole Army, should have withall a peculiar Regiment, or Company of his own. God is King of all the Earth by his Power: but of his chosen people, he is King by Covenant. But to speake more largly of the Kingdome of God, both by Nature, and Covenant, I have in the following discourse assigned an other place.

THE CAUSES OF CHANGE IN RELIGION

From the propagation of Religion, it is not hard to understand the causes of the resolution of the same into its first seeds, or principles; which are only an opinion of a Deity, and Powers invisible, and supernaturall; that can never be so abolished out of humane nature, but that new Religions may againe be made to spring out of them, by the culture of such men, as for such purpose are in reputation.

For seeing all formed Religion, is founded at first, upon the faith which a multitude hath in some one person, whom they believe not only to be a wise man, and to labour to procure their happiness, but also to be a holy man, to whom God himselfe vouchsafeth to declare his will supernaturally; It followeth necessarily, when they that have the Goverment of Religion, shall come to have either the wisedome of those men, their sincerity, or their love suspected; or that they shall be unable to shew any probable token of divine Revelation; that the Religion which they desire to uphold, must be suspected likewise; and (without the feare of the Civill Sword) contradicted and rejected.

INJOYNING BELEEFE OF IMPOSSIBILITIES

That which taketh away the reputation of Wisedome, in him that formeth a Religion, or addeth to it when it is allready formed, is the enjoyning of a beliefe of contradictories: For both parts of a contradiction cannot possibly be true: and therefore to enjoyne the beliefe of them, is an argument of ignorance; which detects the Author in that; and discredits him in all things else he shall propound as from revelation supernaturall: which revelation a man may indeed have of many things above, but of nothing against naturall reason.

DOING CONTRARY TO THE RELIGION THEY ESTABLISH

That which taketh away the reputation of Sincerity, is the doing, or saying of such things, as appeare to be signes, that what they require other men to believe, is not believed by themselves; all which doings, or sayings are therefore called Scandalous, because they be stumbling blocks, that make men to fall in the way of Religion: as Injustice, Cruelty, Prophanesse, Avarice, and Luxury. For who can believe, that he that doth ordinarily such actions, as proceed from any of these rootes, believeth there is any such Invisible Power to be feared, as he affrighteth other men withall, for lesser faults?

That which taketh away the reputation of Love, is the being detected of private ends: as when the beliefe they require of others, conduceth or seemeth to conduce to the acquiring of Dominion, Riches, Dignity, or secure Pleasure, to themselves onely, or specially. For that which men reap benefit by to themselves, they are thought to do for their own sakes, and not for love of others

WANT OF THE TESTIMONY OF MIRACLES

Lastly, the testimony that men can render of divine Calling, can be no other, than the operation of Miracles; or true Prophecy, (which also is a Miracle;) or extraordinary Felicity. And therefore, to those points of Religion, which have been received from them that did such Miracles; those that are added by such, as approve not their Calling by some Miracle, obtain no greater beliefe, than what the Custome, and Lawes of the places, in which they be educated, have wrought into them. For as in naturall things, men of judgement require naturall signes, and arguments; so in supernaturall things, they require signes supernaturall, (which are Miracles,) before they consent inwardly, and from their hearts.

All which causes of the weakening of mens faith, do manifestly appear in the Examples following. First, we have the Example of the children of Israel; who when Moses, that had approved his Calling to them by Miracles, and by the happy conduct of them out of Egypt, was absent but 40 dayes, revolted from the worship of the true God, recommended to them by him; and setting up (Exod.32 1,2) a Golden Calfe for their God, relapsed into the Idolatry of the Egyptians; from whom they had been so lately delivered. And again, after Moses, Aaron, Joshua, and that generation which had seen the great works of God in Israel, (Judges 2 11) were dead; another generation arose, and served Baal. So that Miracles fayling, Faith also failed.

Again, when the sons of Samuel, (1 Sam.8.3) being constituted by their father Judges in Bersabee, received bribes, and judged unjustly, the people of Israel refused any more to have God to be their King, in other manner than he was King of other people; and therefore cryed out to Samuel, to choose them a King after the manner of the Nations. So that Justice Fayling, Faith also fayled: Insomuch, as they deposed their God, from reigning over them.

And whereas in the planting of Christian Religion, the Oracles ceased in all parts of the Roman Empire, and the number of Christians encreased wonderfully every day, and in every place, by the preaching of the Apostles, and Evangelists; a great part of that successe, may reasonably be attributed, to the contempt, into which the Priests of the Gentiles of that time, had brought themselves, by their uncleannesse, avarice, and jugling between Princes. Also the Religion of the Church of Rome, was partly, for the same cause abolished in England, and many other parts of Christendome; insomuch, as the fayling of Vertue in the Pastors, maketh Faith faile in the People:

and partly from bringing of the Philosophy, and doctrine of Aristotle into Religion, by the Schoole-men; from whence there arose so many contradictions, and absurdities, as brought the Clergy into a reputation both of Ignorance, and of Fraudulent intention; and enclined people to revolt from them, either against the will of their own Princes, as in France, and Holland; or with their will, as in England.

Lastly, amongst the points by the Church of Rome declared necessary for Salvation, there be so many, manifestly to the advantage of the Pope, and of his spirituall subjects, residing in the territories of other Christian Princes, that were it not for the mutuall emulation of those Princes, they might without warre, or trouble, exclude all forraign Authority, as easily as it has been excluded in England. For who is there that does not see, to whose benefit it conduceth, to have it believed, that a King hath not his Authority from Christ, unlesse a Bishop crown him? That a King, if he be a Priest, cannot Marry? That whether a Prince be born in lawfull Marriage, or not, must be judged by Authority from Rome? That Subjects may be freed from their Alleageance, if by the Court of Rome, the King be judged an Heretique? That a King (as Chilperique of France) may be deposed by a Pope (as Pope Zachary,) for no cause; and his Kingdome given to one of his Subjects? That the Clergy, and Regulars, in what Country soever, shall be exempt from the Jurisdiction of their King, in cases criminall? Or who does not see, to whose profit redound the Fees of private Masses, and Vales of Purgatory; with other signes of private interest, enough to mortifie the most lively Faith, if (as I sayd) the civill Magistrate, and Custome did not more sustain it, than any opinion they have of the Sanctity, Wisdome, or Probity of their Teachers? So that I may attribute all the changes of Religion in the world, to one and the some cause; and that is, unpleasing Priests; and those not onely amongst Catholiques, but even in that Church that hath presumed most of Reformation.

CHAPTER THIRTEEN

Of the Naturall Condition of Mankind, as Concerning their Felicity, and Misery

NATURE HATH MADE MEN so equall, in the faculties of body, and mind; as that though there bee found one man sometimes manifestly stronger in body, or of quicker mind then another; yet when all is reckoned together, the difference between man, and man, is not so considerable, as that one man can thereupon claim to himselfe any benefit, to which another may not pretend, as well as he. For as to the strength of body, the weakest has strength enough to kill the strongest, either by secret machination, or by confederacy with others, that are in the same danger with himselfe.

And as to the faculties of the mind, (setting aside the arts grounded upon words, and especially that skill of proceeding upon generall, and infallible rules, called Science; which very few have, and but in few things; as being not a native faculty, born with us; nor attained, (as Prudence,) while we look after somewhat els,) I find yet a greater equality amongst men, than that of strength. For Prudence, is but Experience; which equall time, equally bestowes on all men, in those things they equally apply themselves unto. That which may perhaps make such equality incredible, is but a vain conceipt of ones owne wisdome, which almost all men think they have in a greater degree, than the Vulgar; that is, than all men but themselves, and a few others, whom by Fame, or for concurring with themselves, they approve. For such is the nature of men, that howsoever they may acknowledge many others to be more witty, or more eloquent, or more learned; Yet they will hardly believe there be many so wise as themselves: For they see their own wit at hand, and other mens at a distance. But this proveth rather that men are in that point equall, than unequall. For there is not ordinarily a greater signe of the equall distribution of any thing, than that every man is contented with his share.

FROM EQUALITY PROCEEDS DIFFIDENCE

From this equality of ability, ariseth equality of hope in the attaining of our Ends. And therefore if any two men desire the same thing, which neverthelesse they cannot both enjoy, they become enemies; and in the way to their End, (which is principally their owne conservation, and sometimes their delectation only,) endeavour to destroy, or subdue one an other. And from hence it comes to passe, that where an Invader hath no more to feare, than an other mans single power; if one plant, sow, build, or possesse a convenient Seat, others may probably be expected to come prepared with forces united, to dispossesse, and deprive him, not only of the fruit of his labour, but also of his life, or liberty. And the Invader again is in the like danger of another.

FROM DIFFIDENCE WARRE

And from this diffidence of one another, there is no way for any man to secure himselfe, so reasonable, as Anticipation; that is, by force, or wiles, to master the persons of all men he can, so long, till he see no other power great enough to endanger him: And this is no more than his own conservation requireth, and is generally allowed. Also because there be some, that taking pleasure in contemplating their own power in the acts of conquest, which they pursue farther than their security requires; if others, that otherwise would be glad to be at ease within modest bounds, should not by invasion increase their power, they would not be able, long time, by standing only on their defence, to subsist. And by consequence, such augmentation of dominion over men, being necessary to a mans conservation, it ought to be allowed him.

Againe, men have no pleasure, (but on the contrary a great deale of griefe) in keeping company, where there is no power able to over-awe them all. For every man looketh that his companion should value him, at the same rate he sets upon himselfe: And upon all signes of contempt, or undervaluing, naturally endeavours, as far as he dares (which amongst them that have no common power, to keep them in quiet, is far enough to make them destroy each other,) to extort a greater value from his contemners, by dommage; and from others, by the example.

So that in the nature of man, we find three principall causes of quarrel. First, Competition; Secondly, Diffidence; Thirdly, Glory.

The first, maketh men invade for Gain; the second, for Safety; and the third, for Reputation. The first use Violence, to make themselves Masters of other mens persons, wives, children, and cattell; the second, to defend them; the third, for trifles, as a word, a smile, a different opinion, and any other signe of undervalue, either direct in their Persons, or by reflexion in their Kindred, their Friends, their Nation, their Profession, or their Name.

OUT OF CIVIL STATES,

There Is Alwayes Warre Of Every One Against Every One Hereby it is manifest, that during the time men live without a common Power to keep them all in awe, they are in that condition which is called Warre; and such a warre, as is of every man, against every man. For WARRE, consisteth not in Battell onely, or the act of fighting; but in a tract of time, wherein the Will to contend by Battell is sufficiently known: and therefore the notion of Time, is to be considered in the nature of Warre; as it is in the nature of Weather. For as the nature of Foule weather, lyeth not in a showre or two of rain; but in an inclination thereto of many dayes together: So the nature of War, consisteth not in actuall fighting; but in the known disposition thereto, during all the time there is no assurance to the contrary. All other time is PEACE.

THE INCOMMODITES OF SUCH A WAR

Whatsoever therefore is consequent to a time of Warre, where every man is Enemy to every man; the same is consequent to the time, wherein men live without other security, than what their own strength, and their own invention shall furnish them withall. In such condition, there is no place for Industry; because the fruit thereof is uncertain; and consequently no Culture of the Earth; no Navigation, nor use of the commodities that may be imported by Sea; no commodious Building; no Instruments of moving, and removing such things as require much force; no Knowledge of the face of the Earth; no account of Time; no Arts; no Letters; no Society; and which is worst of all, continuall feare, and danger of violent death; And the life of man, solitary, poore, nasty, brutish, and short.

It may seem strange to some man, that has

not well weighed these things; that Nature should thus dissociate, and render men apt to invade, and destroy one another: and he may therefore, not trusting to this Inference, made from the Passions, desire perhaps to have the same confirmed by Experience. Let him therefore consider with himselfe, when taking a journey, he armes himselfe, and seeks to go well accompanied; when going to sleep, he locks his dores; when even in his house he locks his chests; and this when he knows there bee Lawes, and publike Officers, armed, to revenge all injuries shall bee done him; what opinion he has of his fellow subjects, when he rides armed; of his fellow Citizens, when he locks his dores; and of his children, and servants, when he locks his chests. Does he not there as much accuse mankind by his actions, as I do by my words? But neither of us accuse mans nature in it. The Desires, and other Passions of man, are in themselves no Sin. No more are the Actions, that proceed from those Passions, till they know a Law that forbids them; which till Lawes be made they cannot know: nor can any Law be made, till they have agreed upon the Person that shall make it.

It may peradventure be thought, there was never such a time, nor condition of warre as this; and I believe it was never generally so, over all the world: but there are many places, where they live so now. For the savage people in many places of America, except the government of small Families, the concord whereof dependeth on naturall lust, have no government at all; and live at this day in that brutish manner, as I said before. Howsoever, it may be perceived what manner of life there would be, where there were no common Power to feare; by the manner of life, which men that have formerly lived under a peacefull government, use to degenerate into, in a civill Warre.

But though there had never been any time, wherein particular men were in a condition of warre one against another; yet in all times, Kings, and persons of Soveraigne authority, because of their Independency, are in continuall jealousies, and in the state and posture of Gladiators; having their weapons pointing, and their eyes fixed on one another; that is, their Forts, Garrisons, and Guns upon the Frontiers of their Kingdomes; and continuall Spyes upon their neighbours; which is a posture of War. But because they uphold thereby, the Industry of their Subjects; there does not follow from it, that misery, which accompanies the Liberty of particular men.

IN SUCH A WARRE, NOTHING IS UNJUST

To this warre of every man against every man, this also is consequent; that nothing can be Unjust. The notions of Right and Wrong, Justice and Injustice have there no place. Where there is no common Power, there is no Law: where no Law, no Injustice. Force, and Fraud, are in warre the two Cardinall vertues. Justice, and Injustice are none of the Faculties neither of the Body, nor Mind. If they were, they might be in a man that were alone in the world, as well as his Senses, and Passions. They are Qualities, that relate to men in Society, not in Solitude. It is consequent also to the same condition, that there be no Propriety, no Dominion, no Mine and Thine distinct; but onely that to be every mans that he can get; and for so long, as he can keep it. And thus much for the ill condition, which man by meer Nature is actually placed in; though with a possibility to come out of it, consisting partly in the Passions, partly in his Reason.

THE PASSIONS THAT INCLINE MEN TO PEACE

The Passions that encline men to Peace, are Feare of Death; Desire of such things as are necessary to commodious living; and a Hope by their Industry to obtain them. And Reason suggesteth convenient Articles of Peace, upon which men may be drawn to agreement. These Articles, are they, which otherwise are called the Lawes of Nature: whereof I shall speak more particularly, in the two following Chapters.

CHAPTER FOURTEEN

Of the First and Second Naturall Lawes, and of Contracts

RIGHT OF NATURE WHAT

THE RIGHT OF NATURE, which Writers commonly call Jus Naturale, is the Liberty each man hath, to use his own power, as he will himselfe, for the preservation of his own

Nature; that is to say, of his own Life; and consequently, of doing any thing, which in his own Judgement, and Reason, hee shall conceive to be the aptest means thereunto.

LIBERTY WHAT

By LIBERTY, is understood, according to the proper signification of the word, the absence of externall Impediments: which Impediments, may oft take away part of a mans power to do what hee would; but cannot hinder him from using the power left him, according as his judgement, and reason shall dictate to him.

A LAW OF NATURE WHAT

A LAW OF NATURE, (Lex Naturalis,) is a Precept, or generall Rule, found out by Reason, by which a man is forbidden to do, that, which is destructive of his life, or taketh away the means of preserving the same; and to omit, that, by which he thinketh it may be best preserved. For though they that speak of this subject, use to confound Jus, and Lex, Right and Law; yet they ought to be distinguished; because RIGHT, consisteth in liberty to do, or to forbeare; Whereas LAW, determineth, and bindeth to one of them: so that Law, and Right, differ as much, as Obligation, and Liberty; which in one and the same matter are inconsistent.

NATURALLY EVERY MAN HAS RIGHT TO EVERYTHING

And because the condition of Man, (as hath been declared in the precedent Chapter) is a condition of Warre of every one against every one; in which case every one is governed by his own Reason; and there is nothing he can make use of, that may not be a help unto him, in preserving his life against his enemyes; It followeth, that in such a condition, every man has a Right to every thing; even to one anothers body. And therefore, as long as this naturall Right of every man to every thing endureth, there can be no security to any man, (how strong or wise soever he be,) of living out the time, which Nature ordinarily alloweth men to live.

THE FUNDAMENTAL LAW OF NATURE

And consequently it is a precept, or generall rule of Reason, "That every man, ought to endeavour Peace, as farre as he has hope of obtaining it; and when he cannot obtain it, that he may seek, and use, all helps, and advantages of Warre." The first branch, of which Rule, containeth the first, and Fundamentall Law of Nature; which is, "To seek Peace, and follow it." The Second, the summe of the Right of Nature; which is, "By all means we can, to defend our selves."

THE SECOND LAW OF NATURE

From this Fundamentall Law of Nature, by which men are commanded to endeavour Peace, is derived this second Law; "That a man be willing, when others are so too, as farre-forth, as for Peace, and defence of himselfe he shall think it necessary, to lay down this right to all things; and be contented with so much liberty against other men, as he would allow other men against himselfe." For as long as every man holdeth this Right, of doing any thing he liketh; so long are all men in the condition of Warre. But if other men will not lay down their Right, as well as he; then there is no Reason for any one, to devest himselfe of his: For that were to expose himselfe to Prey, (which no man is bound to) rather than to dispose himselfe to Peace. This is that Law of the Gospell; "Whatsoever you require that others should do to you, that do ye to them." And that Law of all men, "Quod tibi feiri non vis, alteri ne feceris."

WHAT IT IS TO LAY DOWN A RIGHT

To Lay Downe a mans Right to any thing, is to Devest himselfe of the Liberty, of hindring another of the benefit of his own Right to the same. For he that renounceth, or passeth away his Right, giveth not to any other man a Right which he had not before; because there is nothing to which every man had not Right by Nature: but onely standeth out of his way, that he may enjoy his own originall Right, without hindrance from him; not without hindrance from another. So that the effect which redoundeth to one man, by another mans defect of Right, is but so much diminution of impediments to the use of his own Right originall.

RENOUNCING (OR) TRANSFERRING RIGHT WHAT; OBLIGATION DUTY JUSTICE

Right is layd aside, either by simply Renouncing it; or by Transferring it to another. By Simply RENOUNCING; when he cares not to whom the benefit thereof redoundeth. By TRANSFERRING; when he intendeth the benefit thereof to some certain person, or persons. And when a man hath in either manner abandoned, or granted away his Right; then is he said to be OBLIGED, or BOUND, not to hinder those, to whom such Right is granted, or abandoned, from the benefit of it: and that he Ought, and it his DUTY, not to make voyd that voluntary act of his own: and that such hindrance is INJUSTICE, and INJURY, as being Sine Jure; the Right being before renounced, or transferred. So that Injury, or Injustice, in the controversies of the world, is somewhat like to that, which in the disputations of Scholers is called Absurdity. For as it is there called an Absurdity, to contradict what one maintained in the Beginning: so in the world, it is called Injustice, and Injury, voluntarily to undo that, which from the beginning he had voluntarily done. The way by which a man either simply Renounceth, or Transferreth his Right, is a Declaration, or Signification, by some voluntary and sufficient signe, or signes, that he doth so Renounce, or Transferre; or hath so Renounced, or Transferred the same, to him that accepteth it. And these Signes are either Words onely, or Actions onely; or (as it happeneth most often) both Words and Actions. And the same are the BONDS, by which men are bound, and obliged: Bonds, that have their strength, not from their own Nature, (for nothing is more easily broken then a mans word,) but from Feare of some evill consequence upon the rupture.

NOT ALL RIGHTS ARE ALIENABLE

Whensoever a man Transferreth his Right, or Renounceth it; it is either in consideration of some Right reciprocally transferred to himselfe; or for some other good he hopeth for thereby. For it is a voluntary act: and of the voluntary acts of every man, the object is some Good To Himselfe. And therefore there be some Rights, which no man can be understood by any words, or other signes, to have abandoned, or transferred. As first a man cannot lay down the right of resisting them, that assault him by force, to take away his life; because he cannot be understood to ayme thereby, at any Good to himselfe. The same may be sayd of Wounds, and Chayns, and Imprisonment; both because there is no benefit consequent to such patience; as there is to the patience of suffering another to be wounded, or imprisoned: as also because a man cannot tell, when he seeth men proceed against him by violence, whether they intend his death or not. And lastly the motive, and end for which this renouncing, and transferring or Right is introduced, is nothing else but the security of a mans person, in his life, and in the means of so preserving life, as not to be weary of it. And therefore if a man by words, or other signes, seem to despoyle himselfe of the End, for which those signes were intended; he is not to be understood as if he meant it, or that it was his will; but that he was ignorant of how such words and actions were to be interpreted.

CONTRACT WHAT

THE MUTUALL TRANSFERRING OF RIGHT, IS THAT WHICH MEN CALL CONTRACT.

There is difference, between transferring of Right to the Thing; and transferring, or tradition, that is, delivery of the Thing it selfe. For the Thing may be delivered together with the Translation of the Right; as in buying and selling with ready mony; or exchange of goods, or lands: and it may be delivered some time after.

COVENANT WHAT

Again, one of the Contractors, may deliver the Thing contracted for on his part, and leave the other to perform his part at some determinate time after, and in the mean time be trusted; and then the Contract on his part, is called PACT, or COVENANT: Or both parts may contract now, to performe hereafter: in which cases, he that is to performe in time to come, being trusted, his performance is called Keeping Of Promise, or Faith; and the fayling of performance (if it be voluntary) Violation Of Faith.

FREE-GIFT

When the transferring of Right, is not mutuall; but one of the parties transferreth, in hope to gain thereby friendship, or service from another, or from his friends; or in hope to gain the reputation of Charity, or Magnanimity; or to deliver his mind from the pain of compassion; or in hope of reward in heaven; This is not Contract, but GIFT, FREEGIFT, GRACE: which words signifie one and the same thing.

SIGNES OF CONTRACT EXPRESSE

Signes of Contract, are either Expresse, or By Inference. Expresse, are words spoken with understanding of what they signifie; And such words are either of the time Present, or Past; as, I Give, I Grant, I Have Given, I Have Granted, I Will That This Be Yours: Or of the future; as, I Will Give, I Will Grant; which words of the future, are called Promise.

SIGNES OF CONTRACT BY INFERENCE

Signes by Inference, are sometimes the consequence of Words; sometimes the consequence of Silence; sometimes the consequence of Actions; sometimes the consequence of Forbearing an Action: and generally a signe by Inference, of any Contract, is whatsoever sufficiently argues the will of the Contractor.

FREE GIFT PASSETH BY WORDS OF THE PRESENT OR PAST

Words alone, if they be of the time to come, and contain a bare promise, are an insufficient signe of a Free-gift and therefore not obligatory. For if they be of the time to Come, as, To Morrow I Will Give, they are a signe I have not given yet, and consequently that my right is not transferred, but remaineth till I transferre it by some other Act. But if the words be of the time Present, or Past, as, "I have given, or do give to be delivered to morrow," then is my to morrows Right given away to day; and that by the vertue of the words, though there were no other argument of my will. And there is a great difference in the signification of these words, Volos Hoc Tuum Esse Cras, and Cros Dabo; that is between "I will that this be thine to morrow," and, "I will give it to thee to morrow:" For the word I Will, in the former manner of speech, signifies an act of the will Present; but in the later, it signifies a promise of an act of the will to Come: and therefore the former words, being of the Present, transferre a future right; the later, that be of the Future, transferre nothing. But if there be other signes of the Will to transferre a Right, besides Words; then, though the gift be Free, yet may the Right be understood to passe by words of the future: as if a man propound a Prize to him that comes first to the end of a race, The gift is Free; and though the words be of the Future, yet the Right passeth: for if he would not have his words so be understood, he should not have let them runne.

Signes Of Contract Are Words Both Of The Past, Present, and Future In Contracts, the right passeth, not onely where the words are of the time Present, or Past; but also where they are of the Future; because all Contract is mutuall translation, or change of Right; and therefore he that promiseth onely, because he hath already received the benefit for which he promiseth, is to be understood as if he intended the Right should passe: for unlesse he had been content to have his words so understood, the other would not have performed his part first. And for that cause, in buying, and selling, and other acts of Contract, A Promise is equivalent to a Covenant; and therefore obligatory.

MERIT WHAT

He that performeth first in the case of a Contract, is said to MERIT that which he is to receive by the performance of the other; and he hath it as Due. Also when a Prize is propounded to many, which is to be given to him onely that winneth; or mony is thrown amongst many, to be enjoyed by them that catch it; though this be a Free Gift; yet so to Win, or so to Catch, is to Merit, and to have it as DUE. For the Right is transferred in the Propounding of the Prize, and in throwing down the mony; though it be not determined to whom, but by the Event of the contention. But there is between these two sorts of Merit, this difference, that In Contract, I Merit by vertue of my own power, and the Contractors need; but in this case of Free Gift, I am enabled to Merit onely by the benignity of the Giver; In Contract, I merit at The Contractors hand that hee should depart with his right; In this case of gift, I Merit not that the giver should part with his right; but that when he has parted with it, it should be mine, rather than anothers. And this I think to be the meaning of that distinction of the Schooles, between Meritum Congrui, and Meritum Condigni. For God Almighty, having promised Paradise to those men (hoodwinkt with carnall desires,) that can walk through this world according to the Precepts, and Limits prescribed by him; they say, he that shall so walk, shall Merit Paradise Ex Congruo. But because no man can demand a right to it, by his own Righteousnesse, or any other power in himselfe, but by the Free Grace of God onely; they say, no man can Merit Paradise Ex Condigno. This I say, I think is the meaning of that distinction; but because Disputers do not agree upon the signification of their own termes of Art, longer than it serves their turn; I will not affirme any thing of their meaning: onely this I say; when a gift is given indefinitely, as a prize to be contended for, he that winneth Meriteth, and may claime the Prize as Due.

COVENANTS OF MUTUALL TRUST, WHEN INVALID

If a Covenant be made, wherein neither of the parties performe presently, but trust one another; in the condition of meer Nature, (which is a condition of Warre of every man against every man,) upon any reasonable suspition, it is Voyd; But if there be a common Power set over them bothe, with right and force sufficient to compell performance; it is not Voyd. For he that performeth first, has no assurance the other will performe after; because the bonds of words are too weak to bridle mens ambition, avarice, anger, and other Passions, without the feare of some coerceive Power; which in the condition of meer Nature, where all men are equall, and judges of the justnesse of their own fears cannot possibly be supposed. And therefore he which performeth first, does but betray himselfe to his enemy; contrary to the Right (he can never abandon) of defending his life, and means of living.

But in a civill estate, where there is a Power set up to constrain those that would otherwise violate their faith, that feare is no more reasonable; and for that cause, he which by the Covenant is to perform first, is obliged so to do.

The cause of Feare, which maketh such a

Covenant invalid, must be alwayes something arising after the Covenant made; as some new fact, or other signe of the Will not to performe; else it cannot make the Covenant Voyd. For that which could not hinder a man from promising, ought not to be admitted as a hindrance of performing.

RIGHT TO THE END, CONTAINETH RIGHT TO THE MEANS

He that transferreth any Right, transferreth the Means of enjoying it, as farre as lyeth in his power. As he that selleth Land, is understood to transferre the Herbage, and whatsoever growes upon it; Nor can he that sells a Mill turn away the Stream that drives it. And they that give to a man The Right of government in Soveraignty, are understood to give him the right of levying mony to maintain Souldiers; and of appointing Magistrates for the administration of Justice.

NO COVENANT WITH BEASTS

To make Covenant with bruit Beasts, is impossible; because not understanding our speech, they understand not, nor accept of any translation of Right; nor can translate any Right to another; and without mutuall acceptation, there is no Covenant.

NOR WITH GOD WITHOUT SPECIALL REVELATION

To make Covenant with God, is impossible, but by Mediation of such as God speaketh to, either by Revelation supernaturall, or by his Lieutenants that govern under him, and in his Name; For otherwise we know not whether our Covenants be accepted, or not. And therefore they that Vow any thing contrary to any law of Nature, Vow in vain; as being a thing unjust to pay such Vow. And if it be a thing commanded by the Law of Nature, it is not the Vow, but the Law that binds them.

NO COVENANT, BUT OF POSSIBLE AND FUTURE

The matter, or subject of a Covenant, is alwayes something that falleth under deliberation; (For to Covenant, is an act of the Will; that is to say an act, and the last act, of deliberation;) and is therefore alwayes understood to be something to come; and which is judged Possible for him that Covenanteth, to performe.

And therefore, to promise that which is known to be Impossible, is no Covenant. But if that prove impossible afterwards, which before was thought possible, the Covenant is valid, and bindeth, (though not to the thing it selfe,) yet to the value; or, if that also be impossible, to the unfeigned endeavour of performing as much as is possible; for to more no man can be obliged.

COVENANTS HOW MADE VOYD

Men are freed of their Covenants two wayes; by Performing; or by being Forgiven. For Performance, is the naturall end of obligation; and Forgivenesse, the restitution of liberty; as being a retransferring of that Right, in which the obligation consisted.

COVENANTS EXTORTED BY FEARE ARE VALIDE

Covenants entred into by fear, in the condition of meer Nature, are obligatory. For example, if I Covenant to pay a ransome, or service for my life, to an enemy; I am bound by it. For it is a Contract, wherein one receiveth the benefit of life; the other is to receive mony, or service for it; and consequently, where no other Law (as in the condition, of meer Nature) forbiddeth the performance, the Covenant is valid. Therefore Prisoners of warre, if trusted with the payment of their Ransome, are obliged to pay it; And if a weaker Prince, make a disadvantageous peace with a stronger, for feare; he is bound to keep it; unlesse (as hath been sayd before) there ariseth some new, and just cause of feare, to renew the war. And even in Common-wealths, if I be forced to redeem my selfe from a Theefe by promising him mony, I am bound to pay it, till the Civill Law discharge me. For whatsoever I may lawfully do without Obligation, the same I may lawfully Covenant to do through feare: and what I lawfully Covenant, I cannot lawfully break.

THE FORMER COVENANT TO ONE, MAKES VOYD THE LATER TO ANOTHER

A former Covenant, makes voyd a later. For a man that hath passed away his Right to one man to day, hath it not to passe to morrow to another: and therefore the later promise passeth no Right, but is null.

A MANS COVENANT NOT TO DEFEND HIMSELFE, IS VOYD

A Covenant not to defend my selfe from force, by force, is alwayes voyd. For (as I have shewed before) no man can transferre, or lay down his Right to save himselfe from Death, Wounds, and Imprisonment, (the avoyding whereof is the onely End of laying down any Right,) and therefore the promise of not resisting force, in no Covenant transferreth any right; nor is obliging. For though a man may Covenant thus, "Unlesse I do so, or so, kill me;" he cannot Covenant thus "Unless I do so, or so, I will not resist you, when you come to kill me." For man by nature chooseth the lesser evill, which is danger of death in resisting; rather than the greater, which is certain and present death in not resisting. And this is granted to be true by all men, in that they lead Criminals to Execution, and Prison, with armed men, notwithstanding that such Criminals have consented to the Law, by which they are condemned.

NO MAN OBLIGED TO ACCUSE HIMSELFE

A Covenant to accuse ones Selfe, without assurance of pardon, is likewise invalide. For in the condition of Nature, where every man is Judge, there is no place for Accusation: and in the Civill State, the Accusation is followed with Punishment; which being Force, a man is not obliged not to resist. The same is also true, of the Accusation of those, by whose Condemnation a man falls into misery; as of a Father, Wife, or Benefactor. For the Testimony of such an Accuser, if it be not willingly given, is praesumed to be corrupted by Nature; and therefore not to be received: and where a mans Testimony is not to be credited, his not bound to give it. Also Accusations upon Torture, are not to be reputed as Testimonies. For Torture is to be used but as means of conjecture, and light, in the further examination, and search of truth; and what is in that case confessed, tendeth to the ease of him that is Tortured; not to the informing of the Torturers: and therefore ought not to have the credit of a sufficient Testimony: for whether he deliver himselfe by true, or false Accusation, he does it by the Right of preserving his own life.

THE END OF AN OATH; THE FORME OF AS OATH

The force of Words, being (as I have formerly noted) too weak to hold men to the performance of their Covenants; there are in mans nature, but two imaginable helps to strengthen it. And those are either a Feare of the consequence of breaking their word; or a Glory, or Pride in appearing not to need to breake it. This later is a Generosity too rarely found to be presumed on, especially in the pursuers of Wealth, Command, or sensuall Pleasure; which are the greatest part of Mankind. The Passion to be reckoned upon, is Fear; whereof there be two very generall Objects: one, the Power of Spirits Invisible; the other, the Power of those men they shall therein Offend. Of these two, though the former be the greater Power, yet the feare of the later is commonly the greater Feare. The Feare of the former is in every man, his own Religion: which hath place in the nature of man before Civill Society. The later hath not so; at least not place enough, to keep men to their promises; because in the condition of meer Nature, the inequality of Power is not discerned, but by the event of Battell. So that before the time of Civill Society, or in the interruption thereof by Warre, there is nothing can strengthen a Covenant of Peace agreed on, against the temptations of Avarice, Ambition, Lust, or other strong desire, but the feare of that Invisible Power, which they every one Worship as God; and Feare as a Revenger of their perfidy. All therefore that can be done between two men not subject to Civill Power, is to put one another to swear by the God he feareth: Which Swearing or OATH, is a Forme Of Speech, Added To A Promise; By Which He That Promiseth, Signifieth, That Unlesse He Performe, He Renounceth The Mercy Of His God, Or Calleth To Him For Vengeance On Himselfe. Such was the Heathen Forme, "Let Jupiter kill me else, as I kill this Beast." So is our Forme, "I shall do thus, and thus, so help me God." And this, with the Rites and Ceremonies, which every one useth in his own Religion, that the feare of breaking faith might be the greater.

NO OATH, BUT BY GOD

By this it appears, that an Oath taken according to any other Forme, or Rite, then his, that sweareth, is in vain; and no Oath: And there is no Swearing by any thing which the Swearer thinks not God. For though men have sometimes used to swear by their Kings, for feare, or flattery; yet they would have it thereby understood, they attributed to them Divine honour. And that Swearing unnecessarily by God, is but prophaning of his name: and Swearing by other things, as men do in common discourse, is not Swearing, but an impious Custome, gotten by too much vehemence of talking.

AN OATH ADDES NOTHING TO THE OBLIGATION

It appears also, that the Oath addes nothing to the Obligation. For a Covenant, if lawfull, binds in the sight of God, without the Oath, as much as with it; if unlawfull, bindeth not at all; though it be confirmed with an Oath.

CHAPTER FIFTEEN

Of Other Lawes of Nature

THE THIRD LAW OF NATURE, JUSTICE

FROM THAT LAW OF NATURE, by which we are obliged to transferre to another, such Rights, as being retained, hinder the peace of Mankind, there followeth a Third; which is this, That Men Performe Their Covenants Made: without which, Covenants are in vain, and but Empty words; and the Right of all men to all things remaining, wee are still in the condition of Warre.

JUSTICE AND INJUSTICE WHAT

And in this law of Nature, consisteth the Fountain and Originall of JUSTICE. For where no Covenant hath preceded, there hath no Right been transferred, and every man has right to every thing; and consequently, no action can be Unjust. But when a Covenant is made, then to break it is Unjust: And the definition of INJUSTICE, is no other than The Not Performance Of Covenant. And whatsoever is not Unjust, is Just.

Justice And Propriety Begin With The Constitution of Common-wealth But because Covenants of mutuall trust, where there is a feare of not performance on either part, (as hath been said in the former Chapter,) are invalid; though the Originall of Justice be the making of Covenants; yet Injustice actually there can be none, till the cause of such feare be taken away; which while men are in the naturall condition of Warre, cannot be done. Therefore before the names of Just, and Unjust can have place, there must be some coercive Power, to compell men equally to the performance of their Covenants, by the terrour of some punishment, greater than the benefit they expect by the breach of their Covenant; and to make good that Propriety, which by mutuall Contract men acquire, in recompence of the universall Right they abandon: and such power there is none before the erection of a Common-wealth. And this is also to be gathered out of the ordinary definition of Justice in the Schooles: For they say, that "Justice is the constant Will of giving to every man his own." And therefore where there is no Own, that is, no Propriety, there is no Injustice; and where there is no coerceive Power erected, that is, where there is no Common-wealth, there is no Propriety;

all men having Right to all things: Therefore where there is no Common-wealth, there nothing is Unjust. So that the nature of Justice, consisteth in keeping of valid Covenants: but the Validity of Covenants begins not but with the Constitution of a Civill Power, sufficient to compell men to keep them: And then it is also that Propriety begins.

JUSTICE NOT CONTRARY TO REASON

The Foole hath sayd in his heart, there is no such thing as Justice; and sometimes also with his tongue; seriously alleaging, that every mans conservation, and contentment, being committed to his own care, there could be no reason, why every man might not do what he thought conduced thereunto; and therefore also to make, or not make; keep, or not keep Covenants, was not against Reason, when it conduced to ones benefit. He does not therein deny, that there be

Covenants; and that they are sometimes broken, sometimes kept; and that such breach of them may be called Injustice, and the observance of them Justice: but he questioneth, whether Injustice, taking away the feare of God, (for the same Foole hath said in his heart there is no God,) may not sometimes stand with that Reason, which dictateth to every man his own good; and particularly then, when it conduceth to such a benefit, as shall put a man in a condition, to neglect not onely the dispraise, and revilings, but also the power of other men. The Kingdome of God is gotten by violence; but what if it could be gotten by unjust violence? were it against Reason so to get it, when it is impossible to receive hurt by it? and if it be not against Reason, it is not against Justice; or else Justice is not to be approved for good. From such reasoning as this, Succesfull wickednesse hath obtained the Name of Vertue; and some that in all other things have disallowed the violation of Faith; yet have allowed it, when it is for the getting of a Kingdome. And the Heathen that believed, that Saturn was deposed by his son Jupiter, believed neverthelesse the same Jupiter to be the avenger of Injustice: Somewhat like to a piece of Law in Cokes Commentaries on Litleton; where he sayes, If the right Heire of the Crown be attainted of Treason; yet the Crown shall descend to him, and Eo Instante the Atteynder be voyd; From which instances a man will be very prone to inferre; that when the Heire apparent of a Kingdome, shall kill him that is in possession, though his father; you may call it Injustice, or by what other name you will; yet it can never be against Reason, seeing all the voluntary actions of men tend to the benefit of themselves; and those actions are most Reasonable, that conduce most to their ends. This specious reasoning is nevertheless false.

For the question is not of promises mutuall, where there is no security of performance on either side; as when there is no Civill Power erected over the parties promising; for such promises are no Covenants: But either where one of the parties has performed already; or where there is a Power to make him performe; there is the question whether it be against reason, that is, against the benefit of the other to performe, or not. And I say it is not against reason. For the manifestation whereof, we are to consider; First, that when a man doth a thing, which notwithstanding any thing can be foreseen, and reckoned on, tendeth to his own destruction, howsoever some accident which he could not expect, arriving may turne it to his benefit; yet such events do not make it reasonably or wisely done. Secondly, that in a condition of Warre, wherein every man to every man, for want of a common Power to keep them all in awe, is an Enemy, there is no man can hope by his own strength, or wit, to defend himselfe from destruction, without the help of Confederates; where every one expects the same defence by the Confederation, that any one else does: and therefore he which declares he thinks it reason to deceive those that help him, can in reason expect no other means of safety, than what can be had from his own single Power. He therefore that breaketh his Covenant, and consequently declareth that he thinks he may with reason do so, cannot be received into any Society, that unite themselves for Peace and defence, but by the errour of them that receive him; nor when he is received, be retayned in it, without seeing the danger of their errour; which errours a man cannot reasonably reckon upon as the means of his security; and therefore if he be left, or cast out of Society, he perisheth; and if he live in Society, it is by the errours of other men, which he could not foresee, nor reckon upon; and consequently against the reason of his preservation; and so, as all men that contribute not to his destruction, forbear him onely out of ignorance of what is good for themselves.

As for the Instance of gaining the secure and perpetuall felicity of Heaven, by any way; it is frivolous: there being but one way imaginable; and that is not breaking, but keeping of Covenant.

And for the other Instance of attaining Soveraignty by Rebellion; it is manifest, that though the event follow, yet because it cannot reasonably be expected, but rather the contrary; and because by gaining it so, others are taught to gain the same in like manner, the attempt thereof is against reason. Justice therefore, that is to say, Keeping of Covenant, is a Rule of Reason, by which we are forbidden to do any thing destructive to our life; and consequently a Law of Nature.

There be some that proceed further; and will not have the Law of Nature, to be those Rules which conduce to the preservation of mans life on earth; but to the attaining of an eternall felicity after death; to which they think the breach of Covenant may conduce;

and consequently be just and reasonable; (such are they that think it a work of merit to kill, or depose, or rebell against, the Soveraigne Power constituted over them by their own consent.) But because there is no naturall knowledge of mans estate after death; much lesse of the reward that is then to be given to breach of Faith; but onely a beliefe grounded upon other mens saying, that they know it supernaturally, or that they know those, that knew them, that knew others, that knew it supernaturally; Breach of Faith cannot be called a Precept of Reason, or Nature.

COVENANTS NOT DISCHARGED BY THE VICE OF THE PERSON TO WHOM MADE

Others, that allow for a Law of Nature, the keeping of Faith, do neverthelesse make exception of certain persons; as Heretiques, and such as use not to performe their Covenant to others: And this also is against reason. For if any fault of a man, be sufficient to discharge our Covenant made; the same ought in reason to have been sufficient to have hindred the making of it.

JUSTICE OF MEN, AND JUSTICE OF ACTIONS WHAT

The names of Just, and Unjust, when they are attributed to Men, signifie one thing; and when they are attributed to Actions, another. When they are attributed to Men, they signifie Conformity, or Inconformity of Manners, to Reason. But when they are attributed to Actions, they signifie the Conformity, or Inconformity to Reason, not of Manners, or manner of life, but of particular Actions. A Just man therefore, is he that taketh all the care he can, that his Actions may be all Just: and an Unjust man, is he that neglecteth it. And such men are more often in our Language stiled by the names of Righteous, and Unrighteous; then Just, and Unjust; though the meaning be the same. Therefore a Righteous man, does not lose that Title, by one, or a few unjust Actions, that proceed from sudden Passion, or mistake of Things, or Persons: nor does an Unrighteous man, lose his character, for such Actions, as he does, of forbeares to do, for feare: because his Will is not framed by the Justice, but by the apparant benefit of what he is to do. That which gives to humane Actions the relish of Justice, is a certain Noblenesse or Gallantnesse of courage, (rarely found,) by which a man scorns to be beholding for the contentment of his life, to fraud, or breach of promise. This Justice of the Manners, is that which is meant, where Justice is called a Vertue; and Injustice a Vice.

But the Justice of Actions denominates men, not Just, but Guiltlesse; and the Injustice of the same, (which is also called

Injury,) gives them but the name of Guilty.

JUSTICE OF MANNERS, AND JUSTICE OF ACTIONS

Again, the Injustice of Manners, is the disposition, or aptitude to do Injurie; and is Injustice before it proceed to Act; and without supposing any individuall person injured. But the Injustice of an Action, (that is to say Injury,) supposeth an individuall person Injured; namely him, to whom the Covenant was made: And therefore many times the injury is received by one man, when the dammage redoundeth to another. As when The Master commandeth his servant to give mony to a stranger; if it be not done, the Injury is done to the Master, whom he had before Covenanted to obey; but the dammage redoundeth to the stranger, to whom he had no Obligation; and therefore could not Injure him. And so also in Common-wealths, private men may remit to one another their debts; but not robberies or other violences, whereby they are endammaged; because the detaining of Debt, is an Injury to themselves; but Robbery and Violence, are Injuries to the Person of the Common-wealth.

NOTHING DONE TO A MAN, BY HIS OWN CONSENT CAN BE INJURY

Whatsoever is done to a man, conformable to his own Will signified to the doer, is no Injury to him. For if he that doeth it, hath not passed away his originall right to do what he please, by some Antecedent Covenant, there is no breach of Covenant; and therefore no Injury done him. And if he have; then his Will to have it done being signified, is a release of that Covenant; and so again there is no Injury done him.

JUSTICE COMMUTATIVE, AND DISTRIBUTIVE

Justice of Actions, is by Writers divided into Commutative, and Distributive; and the former they say consisteth in proportion Arithmeticall; the later in proportion Geometricall. Commutative therefore, they place in the equality of value of the things contracted for; And Distributive, in the distribution of equall benefit, to men of equall merit. As if it were Injustice to sell dearer than we buy; or to give more to a man than he merits. The value of all things contracted for, is measured by the Appetite of the Contractors: and therefore the just value, is that which they be contented to give. And Merit (besides that which is by Covenant, where the performance on one part, meriteth the performance of the other part, and falls under Justice Commutative, not Distributive,) is not due by Justice; but is rewarded of Grace onely.

And therefore this distinction, in the sense wherein it useth to be expounded, is not right. To speak properly, Commutative Justice, is the Justice of a Contractor; that is, a Performance of Covenant, in Buying, and Selling; Hiring, and Letting to Hire; Lending, and Borrowing; Exchanging, Bartering, and other acts of Contract.

And Distributive Justice, the Justice of an Arbitrator; that is to say, the act of defining what is Just. Wherein, (being trusted by them that make him Arbitrator,) if he performe his Trust, he is said to distribute to every man his own: and his is indeed Just Distribution, and may be called (though improperly) Distributive Justice; but more properly Equity; which also is a Law of Nature, as shall be shewn in due place.

THE FOURTH LAW OF NATURE, GRATITUDE

As Justice dependeth on Antecedent

Covenant; so does Gratitude depend on Antecedent Grace; that is to say, Antecedent Free-gift: and is the fourth Law of Nature; which may be conceived in this Forme, “That a man which receiveth Benefit from another of meer Grace, Endeavour that he which giveth it, have no reasonable cause to repent him of his good will.” For no man giveth, but with intention of Good to himselfe; because Gift is Voluntary; and of all Voluntary Acts, the Object is to every man his own Good; of which if men see they shall be frustrated, there will be no beginning of benevolence, or trust; nor consequently of mutuall help; nor of reconciliation of one man to another; and therefore they are to remain still in the condition of War; which is contrary to the first and Fundamentall Law of Nature, which commandeth men to Seek Peace. The breach of this Law, is called Ingratitude; and hath the same relation to Grace, that Injustice hath to Obligation by Covenant.

THE FIFTH, MUTUALL ACCOMMODATION, OR COMPLEASANCE

A fifth Law of Nature, is COMPLEASANCE; that is to say, "That every man strive to accommodate himselfe to the rest." For the understanding whereof, we may consider, that there is in mens aptnesse to Society; a diversity of Nature, rising from their diversity of Affections; not unlike to that we see in stones brought together for building of an Aedifice. For as that stone which by the asperity, and irregularity of Figure, takes more room from others, than it selfe fills; and for the hardnesse, cannot be easily made plain, and thereby hindereth the building, is by the builders cast away as unprofitable, and troublesome: so also, a man that by asperity of Nature, will strive to retain those things which to himselfe are superfluous, and to others necessary; and for the stubbornness of his Passions, cannot be corrected, is to be left, or cast out of Society, as combersome thereunto. For seeing every man, not onely by Right, but also by necessity of Nature, is supposed to endeavour all he can, to obtain that which is necessary for his conservation; He that shall oppose himselfe against it, for things superfluous, is guilty of the warre that thereupon is to follow; and therefore doth that, which is contrary to the fundamentall Law of Nature, which commandeth To Seek Peace. The observers of this Law, may be called SOCIABLE, (the Latines call them Commodi;) The contrary, Stubborn, Insociable, Froward, Intractable.

THE SIXTH, FACILITY TO PARDON

A sixth Law of Nature is this, "That upon caution of the Future time, a man ought to pardon the offences past of them that repenting, desire it." For PARDON, is nothing but granting of Peace; which though granted to them that persevere in their hostility, be not Peace, but Feare; yet not granted to them that give caution of the Future time, is signe of an aversion to Peace; and therefore contrary to the Law of Nature.

THE SEVENTH, THAT IN REVENGES, MEN RESPECT ONELY THE FUTURE GOOD

A seventh is, " That in Revenges, (that is, retribution of evil for evil,) Men look not at the greatnesse of the evill past, but the greatnesse of the good to follow." Whereby we are forbidden to inflict punishment with any other designe, than for correction of the offender, or direction of others. For this Law is consequent to the next before it, that commandeth Pardon, upon security of the Future Time. Besides, Revenge without respect to the Example, and profit to come, is a triumph, or glorying in the hurt of another, tending to no end; (for the End is alwayes somewhat to Come;) and glorying to no end, is vain-glory, and contrary to reason; and to hurt without reason, tendeth to the introduction of Warre; which is against the Law of Nature; and is commonly stiled by the name of Cruelty.

THE EIGHTH, AGAINST CONTUMELY

And because all signes of hatred, or contempt, provoke to fight; insomuch as most men choose rather to hazard their life, than not to be revenged; we may in the eighth place, for a Law of Nature set down this Precept, "That no man by deed, word, countenance, or gesture, declare Hatred, or Contempt of another." The breach of which Law, is commonly called Contumely.

THE NINTH, AGAINST PRIDE

The question who is the better man, has no place in the condition of meer Nature; where, (as has been shewn before,) all men are equall. The inequallity that now is, has been introduced by the Lawes civill. I know that Aristotle in the first booke of his Politiques, for a foundation of his doctrine, maketh men by Nature, some more worthy to Command, meaning the wiser sort (such as he thought himselfe to be for his Philosophy;) others to Serve, (meaning those that had strong bodies, but were not Philosophers as he;) as if Master and Servant were not introduced by consent of men, but by difference of Wit; which is not only against reason; but also against experience. For there are very few so foolish, that had not rather governe themselves, than be governed by others: Nor when the wise in their own conceit, contend by force, with them who distrust their owne wisdome, do they alwaies, or often, or almost at any time, get the Victory. If Nature therefore have made men equall, that equalitie is to be acknowledged; or if Nature have made men unequall; yet because men that think themselves equall, will not enter into conditions of Peace, but upon Equall termes, such equalitie must be admitted. And therefore for the ninth Law of Nature, I put this, "That every man acknowledge other for his Equall by Nature." The breach of this Precept is Pride.

THE TENTH AGAINST ARROGANCE

On this law, dependeth another, "That at the entrance into conditions of Peace, no man require to reserve to himselfe any Right, which he is not content should be reserved to every one of the rest." As it is necessary for all men that seek peace, to lay down certaine Rights of Nature; that is to say, not to have libertie to do all they list:

so is it necessarie for mans life, to retaine some; as right to governe their owne bodies; enjoy aire, water, motion, waies to go from place to place; and all things else without which a man cannot live, or not live well. If in this case, at the making of Peace, men require for themselves, that which they would not have to be granted to others, they do contrary to the precedent law, that commandeth the acknowledgement of naturall equalitie, and therefore also against the law of Nature. The observers of this law, are those we call Modest, and the breakers Arrogant Men. The Greeks call the violation of this law pleonexia; that is, a desire of more than their share.

THE ELEVENTH EQUITY

Also "If a man be trusted to judge between man and man," it is a precept of the Law of Nature, "that he deale Equally between them." For without that, the Controversies of men cannot be determined but by Warre. He therefore that is partiall in judgment, doth what in him lies, to deterre men from the use of Judges, and Arbitrators; and consequently, (against the fundamentall Lawe of Nature) is the cause of Warre.

The observance of this law, from the equall distribution to each man, of that which in reason belongeth to him, is called EQUITY, and (as I have sayd before) distributive justice: the violation, Acception Of Persons, Prosopolepsia.

THE TWELFTH, EQUALL USE OF THINGS COMMON

And from this followeth another law, "That such things as cannot be divided, be enjoyed in Common, if it can be; and if the quantity of the thing permit, without Stint; otherwise Proportionably to the number of them that have Right." For otherwise the distribution is Unequall, and contrary to Equitie.

THE THIRTEENTH, OF LOT

But some things there be, that can neither be divided, nor enjoyed in common. Then, The Law of Nature, which prescribeth Equity, requireth, "That the Entire Right; or else, (making the use alternate,) the First Possession, be determined by Lot." For equall distribution, is of the Law of Nature; and other means of equall distribution cannot be imagined.

THE FOURTEENTH, OF PRIMOGENITURE, AND FIRST SEISING

Of Lots there be two sorts, Arbitrary, and Naturall. Arbitrary, is that which is agreed on by the Competitors; Naturall, is either Primogeniture, (which the Greek calls Kleronomia, which signifies, Given by Lot;) or First Seisure.

And therefore those things which cannot

be enjoyed in common, nor divided, ought to be adjudged to the First Possessor; and is some cases to the First-Borne, as acquired by Lot.

THE FIFTEENTH, OF MEDIATORS

It is also a Law of Nature, "That all men that mediate Peace, be allowed safe Conduct." For the Law that commandeth Peace, as the End, commandeth Intercession, as the Means; and to Intercession the Means is safe Conduct.

THE SIXTEENTH, OF SUBMISSION TO ARBITREMENT

And because, though men be never so willing to observe these Lawes, there may neverthelesse arise questions concerning a mans action; First, whether it were done, or not done; Secondly (if done) whether against the Law, or not against the Law; the former whereof, is called a question Of Fact; the later a question Of Right; therefore unlesse the parties to the question, Covenant mutually to stand to the sentence of another, they are as farre from Peace as ever. This other, to whose Sentence they submit, is called an ARBITRATOR. And therefore it is of the Law of Nature, "That they that are at controversie, submit their Right to the judgement of an Arbitrator."

THE SEVENTEENTH, NO MAN IS HIS OWN JUDGE

And seeing every man is presumed to do all things in order to his own benefit, no man is a fit Arbitrator in his own cause: and if he were never so fit; yet Equity allowing to each party equall benefit, if one be admitted to be Judge, the other is to be admitted also; & so the controversie, that is, the cause of War, remains, against the Law of Nature.

THE EIGHTEENTH, NO MAN TO BE JUDGE, THAT HAS IN HIM CAUSE OF PARTIALITY

For the same reason no man in any Cause ought to be received for Arbitrator, to whom greater profit, or honour, or pleasure apparently ariseth out of the victory of one party, than of the other: for he hath taken (though an unavoydable bribe, yet) a bribe; and no man can be obliged to trust him. And thus also the controversie, and the condition of War remaineth, contrary to the Law of Nature.

THE NINETEENTH, OF WITNESSE

And in a controversie of Fact, the Judge being to give no more credit to one, than to the other, (if there be no other Arguments) must give credit to a third; or to a third and fourth; or more: For else the question is undecided, and left to force, contrary to the Law of Nature.

These are the Lawes of Nature, dictating Peace, for a means of the conservation of men in multitudes; and which onely concern the doctrine of Civill Society. There be other things tending to the destruction of particular men; as Drunkenness, and all other parts of Intemperance; which may therefore also be reckoned amongst those things which the Law of Nature hath forbidden; but are not necessary to be mentioned, nor are pertinent enough to this place.

A RULE, BY WHICH THE LAWS OF NATURE MAY EASILY BE EXAMINED

And though this may seem too subtile a deduction of the Lawes of Nature, to be taken notice of by all men; whereof the most part are too busie in getting food, and the rest too negligent to understand; yet to leave all men unexcusable, they have been contracted into one easie sum, intelligible even to the meanest capacity; and that is, "Do not that to another, which thou wouldest not have done to thy selfe;" which sheweth him, that he has no more to do in learning the Lawes of Nature, but, when weighing the actions of other men with his own, they seem too heavy, to put them into the other part of the ballance, and his own into their place, that his own passions, and selfe-love, may adde nothing to the weight; and then there is none of these Lawes of Nature that will not appear unto him very reasonable.

THE LAWES OF NATURE OBLIGE IN CONSCIENCE ALWAYES,

But In Effect Then Onely When There Is Security The Lawes of Nature oblige In Foro Interno; that is to say, they bind to a desire they should take place: but In Foro Externo; that is, to the putting them in act, not alwayes. For he that should be modest, and tractable, and performe all he promises, in such time, and place, where no man els should do so, should but make himselfe a prey to others, and procure his own certain ruine, contrary to the ground of all Lawes of Nature, which tend to Natures preservation. And again, he that shall observe the same Lawes towards him, observes them not himselfe, seeketh not Peace, but War; & consequently the destruction of his Nature by Violence.

And whatsoever Lawes bind In Foro Interno, may be broken, not onely by a fact contrary to the Law but also by a fact according to it, in case a man think it contrary. For though his Action in this case, be according to the Law; which where the Obligation is In Foro Interno, is a breach.

THE LAWS OF NATURE ARE ETERNAL;

The Lawes of Nature are Immutable and Eternall, For Injustice, Ingratitude, Arrogance, Pride, Iniquity, Acception of persons, and the rest, can never be made lawfull. For it can never be that Warre shall preserve life, and Peace destroy it.

AND YET EASIE

The same Lawes, because they oblige onely to a desire, and endeavour, I mean an unfeigned and constant endeavour, are easie to be observed. For in that they require nothing but endeavour; he that endeavoureth their performance, fulfilleth them; and he that fulfilleth the Law, is Just.

THE SCIENCE OF THESE LAWES, IS THE TRUE MORALL PHILOSOPHY

And the Science of them, is the true and onely Moral Philosophy. For Morall Philosophy is nothing else but the Science of what is Good, and Evill, in the conversation, and Society of mankind. Good, and Evill, are names that signifie our Appetites, and Aversions; which in different tempers, customes, and doctrines of men, are different: And divers men, differ not onely in their Judgement, on the senses of what is pleasant, and unpleasant to the tast, smell, hearing, touch, and sight; but also of what is conformable, or disagreeable to Reason, in the actions of common life. Nay, the same man, in divers times, differs from himselfe; and one time praiseth, that is, calleth Good, what another time he dispraiseth, and calleth Evil: From whence arise Disputes, Controversies, and at last War. And therefore so long as man is in the condition of meer Nature, (which is a condition of War,) as private Appetite is the measure of Good, and Evill: and consequently all men agree on this, that Peace is Good, and therefore also the way, or means of Peace, which (as I have shewed before) are Justice, Gratitude, Modesty, Equity, Mercy, & the rest of the Laws of Nature, are good; that is to say, Morall Vertues; and their contrarie Vices, Evill. Now the science of Vertue and Vice, is Morall Philosophie; and therfore the true Doctrine of the Lawes of Nature, is the true Morall Philosophie. But the Writers of Morall Philosophie, though they acknowledge the same Vertues and Vices; Yet not seeing wherein consisted their Goodnesse; nor that they come to be praised, as the meanes of peaceable, sociable, and comfortable living; place them in a mediocrity of passions: as if not the Cause, but the Degree of daring, made Fortitude; or not the Cause, but the Quantity of a gift, made Liberality.

These dictates of Reason, men use to call by the name of Lawes; but improperly: for they are but Conclusions, or Theoremes concerning what conduceth to the conservation and defence of themselves; whereas Law, properly is the word of him, that by right hath command over others. But yet if we consider the same Theoremes, as delivered in the word of God, that by right commandeth all things; then are they properly called Lawes.

CHAPTER SIXTEEN

Of Persons, Authors, and Things Personated

A PERSON WHAT

A PERSON, IS HE "whose words or actions are considered, either as his own, or as representing the words or actions of an other man, or of any other thing to whom they are attributed, whether Truly or by Fiction."

PERSON NATURALL, AND ARTIFICIALL

When they are considered as his owne, then is he called a Naturall Person: And when they are considered as representing the words and actions of an other, then is he a Feigned or Artificiall person.

THE WORD PERSON, WHENCE

The word Person is latine: instead whereof the Greeks have Prosopon, which signifies the Face, as Persona in latine signifies the Disguise, or Outward Appearance of a man, counterfeited on the Stage; and somtimes more particularly that part of it, which disguiseth the face, as a Mask or Visard: And from the Stage, hath been translated to any Representer of speech and action, as well in Tribunalls, as Theaters. So that a Person, is the same that an Actor is, both on the Stage and in common Conversation;

and to Personate, is to Act, or Represent himselfe, or an other; and he that acteth another, is said to beare his Person, or act in his name; (in which sence Cicero useth it where he saies, "Unus Sustineo Tres Personas; Mei, Adversarii, & Judicis, I beare three Persons; my own, my Adversaries, and the Judges;") and is called in diverse occasions, diversly; as a Representer, or Representative, a Lieutenant, a Vicar, an Attorney, a Deputy, a Procurator, an Actor, and the like.

ACTOR, AUTHOR; AUTHORITY

Of Persons Artificiall, some have their words and actions Owned by those whom they represent. And then the Person is the Actor; and he that owneth his words and actions, is the AUTHOR: In which case the Actor acteth by Authority. For that which in speaking of goods and possessions, is called an Owner, and in latine Dominus, in

Greeke Kurios; speaking of Actions, is called Author. And as the Right of possession, is called Dominion; so the Right of doing any Action, is called AUTHORITY. So that by Authority, is alwayes understood a Right of doing any act: and Done By Authority, done by Commission, or Licence from him whose right it is.

COVENANTS BY AUTHORITY, BIND THE AUTHOR

From hence it followeth, that when the Actor maketh a Covenant by Authority, he bindeth thereby the Author, no lesse than if he had made it himselfe; and no lesse subjecteth him to all the consequences of the same. And therfore all that hath been said formerly, (Chap. 14) of the nature of Covenants between man and man in their naturall capacity, is true also when they are made by their Actors, Representers, or Procurators, that have authority from them, so far-forth as is in their Commission, but no farther.

And therefore he that maketh a Covenant with the Actor, or Representer, not knowing the Authority he hath, doth it at his own perill. For no man is obliged by a Covenant, whereof he is not Author; nor consequently by a Covenant made against, or beside the Authority he gave.

BUT NOT THE ACTOR

When the Actor doth any thing against the Law of Nature by command of the Author, if he be obliged by former Covenant to obey him, not he, but the Author breaketh the Law of Nature: for though the Action be against the Law of Nature; yet it is not his: but contrarily; to refuse to do it, is against the Law of Nature, that forbiddeth breach of Covenant.

THE AUTHORITY IS TO BE SHEWNE

And he that maketh a Covenant with the Author, by mediation of the Actor, not knowing what Authority he hath, but onely takes his word; in case such Authority be not made manifest unto him upon demand, is no longer obliged: For the Covenant made with the Author, is not valid, without his Counter-assurance. But if he that so Covenanteth, knew before hand he was to expect no other assurance, than the Actors word; then is the Covenant valid; because the Actor in this case maketh himselfe the Author. And therefore, as when the Authority is evident, the Covenant obligeth the Author, not the Actor; so when the Authority is feigned, it obligeth the Actor onely; there being no Author but himselfe.

THINGS PERSONATED, INANIMATE

There are few things, that are uncapable of being represented by Fiction. Inanimate things, as a Church, an Hospital, a Bridge, may be Personated by a Rector, Master, or Overseer. But things Inanimate, cannot be Authors, nor therefore give Authority to their Actors: Yet the Actors may have Authority to procure their maintenance, given them by those that are Owners, or Governours of those things. And therefore, such things cannot be Personated, before there be some state of Civill Government.

IRRATIONAL

Likewise Children, Fooles, and Madmen that have no use of Reason, may be Personated by Guardians, or Curators; but can be no Authors (during that time) of any action done by them, longer then (when they shall recover the use of Reason) they shall judge the same reasonable. Yet during the Folly, he that hath right of governing them, may give Authority to the Guardian. But this again has no place but in a State Civill, because before such estate, there is no Dominion of Persons.

FALSE GODS

An Idol, or meer Figment of the brain, my be Personated; as were the Gods of the Heathen; which by such Officers as the State appointed, were Personated, and held Possessions, and other Goods, and Rights, which men from time to time dedicated, and consecrated unto them. But idols cannot be Authors: for a Idol is nothing. The Authority proceeded from the State: and therefore before introduction of Civill Government, the Gods of the Heathen could not be Personated.

THE TRUE GOD

The true God may be Personated. As he was; first, by Moses; who governed the Israelites, (that were not his, but Gods people,) not in his own name, with Hoc Dicit Moses; but in Gods Name, with Hoc Dicit Dominus. Secondly, by the son of man, his own Son our Blessed Saviour Jesus Christ, that came to reduce the Jewes, and induce all Nations into the Kingdome of his Father; not as of himselfe, but as sent from his Father. And thirdly, by the Holy Ghost, or Comforter, speaking, and working in the Apostles: which Holy Ghost, was a Comforter that came not of himselfe; but was sent, and proceeded from them both.

A MULTITUDE OF MEN, HOW ONE PERSON

A Multitude of men, are made One Person, when they are by one man, or one Person,

Represented; so that it be done with the consent of every one of that Multitude in particular. For it is the Unity of the Representer, not the Unity of the Represented, that maketh the Person One. And it is the Representer that beareth the Person, and but one Person: And Unity, cannot otherwise be understood in Multitude.

EVERY ONE IS AUTHOR

And because the Multitude naturally is not One, but Many; they cannot be understood for one; but many Authors, of every thing their Representative faith, or doth in their name; Every man giving their common Representer, Authority from himselfe in particular; and owning all the actions the Representer doth, in case they give him Authority without stint: Otherwise, when they limit him in what, and how farre he shall represent them, none of them owneth more, than they gave him commission to Act.

AN ACTOR MAY BE MANY MEN MADE ONE BY PLURALITY OF VOYCES

And if the Representative consist of many men, the voyce of the greater number, must be considered as the voyce of them all. For if the lesser number pronounce (for example) in the Affirmative, and the greater in the Negative, there will be Negatives more than enough to destroy the Affirmatives; and thereby the excesse of Negatives, standing uncontradicted, are the onely voyce the Representative hath.

REPRESENTATIVES, WHEN THE NUMBER IS EVEN, UNPROFITABLE

And a Representative of even number, especially when the number is not great, whereby the contradictory voyces are oftentimes equall, is therefore oftentimes mute, and uncapable of Action. Yet in some cases contradictory voyces equall in number, may determine a question; as in condemning, or absolving, equality of votes, even in that they condemne not, do absolve; but not on the contrary condemne, in that they absolve not. For when a Cause is heard; not to condemne, is to absolve; but on the contrary, to say that not absolving, is condemning, is not true. The like it is in a deliberation of executing presently, or deferring till another time; For when the voyces are equall, the not decreeing Execution, is a decree of Dilation.

NEGATIVE VOYCE

Or if the number be odde, as three, or more, (men, or assemblies;) whereof every one has by a Negative Voice, authority to take away the effect of all the Affirmative Voices of the rest, This number is no Representative; because by the diversity of Opinions, and

Interests of men, it becomes oftentimes, and in cases of the greatest consequence, a mute Person, and unapt, as for may things else, so for the government of a Multitude, especially in time of Warre.

Of Authors there be two sorts. The first simply so called; which I have before defined to be him, that owneth the Action of another simply. The second is he, that owneth an Action, or Covenant of another conditionally; that is to say, he undertaketh to do it, if the other doth it not, at, or before a certain time. And these Authors conditionall, are generally called SURETYES, in Latine Fidejussores, and Sponsores; and particularly for Debt, Praedes; and for Appearance before a Judge, or Magistrate, Vades.

CONTINUES IN VOLUME TWO

www.ingramcontent.com/pod-product-compliance
Lightning Source LLC
Chambersburg PA
CBHW020445100426
42812CB00036B/3458/J
* 9 7 8 1 8 3 4 1 2 3 8 0 6 *